**Ed Davis**

**Billie Woods**

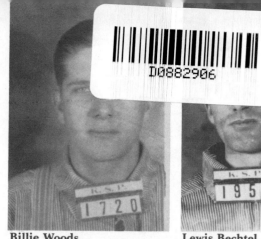

**Lewis Bechtel**

CLARK, JIM                    KSP 2988
EC. 7-8-32    BIRTHDATE 2-6-02
RIME BANK ROBBERY HAB
ENTENCE  LIFE
EIGHT  5' 8"        HAIR   GREY
EIGHT  150          EYES   BLUE
UILD  MEDIUM        RACE   WHITE
EMARKS: REMUGGED  2-25-64

**Jim Clark**

**Bob Brady**

**Kenneth Conn**

**Kenneth Conn**

BAILEY, HARVEY            KSP 3045
REG. 8-17-32  CRIME  BANK ROBBERY
HEIGHT  6'0"          WEIGHT  180 AGE 76
HAIR   GRAY           EYES   BROWN
BUILD  MED_LARGE     RACE   WHITE
SENTENCE  10-50
REMARKS ;  REMUGGED  11-16-62

**Harvey Bailey**

**Wilbur Underhill**

# RUN THE CAT ROADS

To Joe
with best
wishes

L L Edge
May 1983

A True Story of Bank Robbers in the 30's

# RUN THE CAT ROADS

by L.L. Edge

Dembner Books
NEW YORK

Dembner Books
Published by Red Dembner Enterprises Corp., 1841 Broadway,
New York, N.Y. 10023
Distributed by W. W. Norton & Company, Inc., 500 Fifth Avenue,
New York, N.Y. 10110

Library of Congress Cataloging in Publication Data

Edge, L    L
     Run the cat roads.

     1.  Bank robberies—United States—History.
2.  Crime and criminals—United States—History.
I.  Title.
HV6658.E33        346.1′552′0973        80-25930

ISBN 0-934878-01-3

# Contents

A C K N O W L E D G E M E N T S

Grateful acknowledgement is made to the following
sources without which this book could never have been
written: Mary and Harvey Bailey, Hazel and Jim Clark,
Carolyn and Tom Gleason, Frances and Fred Foerschler,
Congressman Wint Smith of Kansas; the staffs of the
public libraries of Dallas, Texas, Kansas City, Kansas, and
Kansas City, Missouri, and of the state historical societies
of California, Kansas, Missouri, and Oklahoma; the more
than twenty newspaper editors and publishers who
cooperated with the use of their files; and, of course, to
my loving wife, Kitty, and three marvelous researchers
and runners, Loy, Jaime, and Jay Edge.

# Preface

Bank robbers made big news in the American Midwest in the nineteen thirties, and one of the biggest stories was the 1933 Memorial Day prison break, when Harvey Bailey, king of the bank robbers, went over the wall of the Kansas State Penitentiary with ten other convicts. The prison was not far from our town, and we all felt the thrill of fear and excitement at the exploit and the ensuing chase.

The next month, an underworld attempt to free another bank robber resulted in a shocking mass murder in nearby Kansas City. And later that summer, bank robbers turned kidnappers and held an Oklahoma oilman for a ransom of two hundred thousand dollars.

This is the true story of those events and the links between them. And it is the story of those times, when criminals had become folk heroes and when men of the law—investigators, enforcement agencies, and prosecutors—were trying desperately to regain the respect of the community.

This book began when I, as a reporter for a daily newspaper, was busy researching another story. Thumbing through some old files, I happened upon the issues covering the prison break. The excitement of those times came flooding back and I determined to find out what I could about them.

It was the start of a long search to dig out the facts from both sides of the law. It took me to the official records and brought me face to face with many of the people in this book. I met Bailey, along in years but sound of mind, with an amazing ability to recall these events of the past. I tracked down Jim Clark and others of the men who had escaped that day. The trail also led to the men who hid them and to those who sought the fugitives, to the biggest figures in the underworld and to the men at the top of the United States Department of Justice and the Federal Bureau of Investigation.

This is not an idle conglomeration of "as told to" reports. It is the product of years of work and travel in a dozen states, of research into official records and personal files, of hundreds of hours of personal interviews.

This book is not what you will find in the official reports. It is not what was reported in the newspapers. But I believe it is the way things really happened.

Let the story speak for itself.

# RUN THE CAT ROADS

## The Massacre

The hot and harried weekend travelers milling about the lobby of Kansas City's Union Station the morning of June 17, 1933, paid scant attention to the arrival of the crack Little Rock Flyer exactly at 7:15 a.m. Two weeks of searing, dry heat with temperatures near the century mark had sent hundreds of city dwellers to seek respite in the cooler rural areas. Mothers dragging small children hustled to catch departing trains, men fanned themselves with straw hats as they waited for their train to be called. But the arrival of the Flyer didn't go unnoticed by two men in a dark-green 1933 Chevrolet coupe parked in front of the station's huge east doors.

Charles Arthur "Pretty Boy" Floyd—a bank robber and bootlegger wanted in six states, the most-publicized criminal of the day—eased open the Chevrolet's door to let air circulate through the car. He shifted the heavy .45-caliber revolver holstered under his left armpit. The second man,

1

Verne Miller, a World War I machine gunner, ex-South Dakota sheriff, bank robber, and professional assassin, had been hired to do a job that might well involve shooting. Floyd, who had arrived in Kansas City only the night before, had been drafted to help.

Using a beefy forefinger as a wiper, Floyd swept beads of perspiration from his forehead. To the southeast, the sun was peeking over Signboard Hill.

"It's gonna be another hot one," Floyd said. "Let's get this damn thing over with in a hurry. It ain't exactly my line of work."

Miller peered intently at a big clock, pedestaled in front of the station doors, before answering.

"Right on time," he noted, referring to the Flyer. "Hell, Charlie, this shouldn't take two minutes—unless some dumb cop starts something."

Floyd grunted in agreement, adjusting another .45 revolver, this one tucked in his trousers waistband. His once-white shirt showed sweat stains entirely around the collar, and a tightly knotted tie drooped carelessly across his large chest. He was five foot ten, the same as his companion, but weighed almost two hundred pounds. His heavy sweating was caused by a combination of the morning heat, already at the 80-degree mark, and a hideous hangover. Despite the heat, Floyd kept his suit coat on to hide his guns. Miller had removed his coat and flung it over the seat between them.

Meanwhile, the Flyer squealed to a halt in the sheds below the main lobby. Four men, one manacled, stood in the vestibule of one of the coach cars, waiting to disembark. Agents Frank Smith and F. J. Lackey of the Federal Bureau of Investigation, Police Chief Otto Reed of McAlester, Oklahoma, and Frank Nash, their prisoner, waited for the porter to clang open the iron door.

Nash, a native of Hobart, Oklahoma, had been among the more successful train robbers in the 1920s, then switched to banks. He was caught, sent to the federal penitentiary at Leavenworth, Kansas, in 1928, but escaped in 1930. This morning, three years later, he was on his way back. The short, stocky outlaw had been recaptured the previous day, June 16, in Hot Springs, Arkansas, by the three men now guarding him and by Joe Ellis, a special agent for the Missouri-Kansas-Texas Railroad.

When Ellis first heard that Nash was hiding in Hot Springs, he enlisted the aid of Reed, who had run up against Nash in Oklahoma. Reed was known as a tough, totally incorruptible officer. After the arrest of Nash, Ellis, who was on vacation, decided to stay in Hot Springs, so Reed agreed to accompany the agents and Nash back to Leavenworth. From Kansas City, the group planned to travel the final thirty miles to the penitentiary by car.

When the porter opened the trap door above the steps, Smith and Lackey, carrying shotguns, descended to the platform, followed by Nash. Reed, his hand on the butt of his .38 revolver, was last, always remaining behind prisoners he escorted. The group strode hurriedly toward the stairwell leading to the lobby above. At the top of the stairs were two Kansas City Police Department detectives, Frank Hermanson and W. J. "Red" Grooms, and two Kansas City-based FBI agents, Raymond J. Caffrey and R. E. Vetterli.

The detectives were two of the honest officers on the graft-ridden police force. The department was loaded with appointments of the corrupt Pendergast political organization, ranging from the patrolman ranks to city hall. In fact, more than sixty officers had criminal records. Less than half the force was considered honest; the rest were either on the take or under the direct supervision of Johnny Lazia, the North End boss who ran the town. Tom Pendergast pulled the city's political strings, but it was Lazia and his strong-arm men who controlled the police and local crime.

As the seven lawmen hustled the prisoner toward the

east Union Station doors, not even Nash was aware a dangerous bank robber and a cold-blooded professional killer were waiting nearby, ready to free him. Outside, the instant Miller spotted the officers and Nash exiting the doors, he reached for a Thompson submachine gun on the car floorboards. It was 7:18 a.m.

"They're headed for the front row of cars," Miller whispered, fingering the trigger of the machine gun. Floyd eased the .45 from his waistband with his left hand, unconsciously checked the holstered gun with his right.

Suddenly, the officers halted beside a 1931 Chevrolet with Nebraska license plates. Lackey, Smith, and Reed quickly entered the two-door sedan's back seat. Nash was instructed to sit in the center front seat. Caffrey stood by the driver's door. The Chevrolet was Caffrey's personal auto, chosen rather than a government car to avoid attention. Vetterli moved to the right door where Grooms and Hermanson were standing, their rifles leaning against the car's fender. Their escort car was parked alongside.

"Let's go," Miller ordered. He and Floyd leaped from the coupe, strode twenty feet, and faced the milling officers.

"Up, Up. Get 'em up," Miller screamed.

Grooms, Hermanson, Vetterli, and Caffrey turned to see Miller pointing the submachine gun at them, and Floyd with twin .45s drawn. Inside the car, Reed, Lackey, and Smith peered through the windshield. Nash, instantly realizing he was being rescued, started to slide out Caffrey's side of the car. Suddenly, an ear-splitting shot tore the morning air. Nash jerked forward, slamming into the dashboard, the back of his head blown off. Chief Reed, his smoking .38 still in his right hand, turned the weapon toward Miller, who was less than ten feet in front of the car. Miller's machine gun erupted before Reed could pull the trigger. Two bullets ripped through the officer's head and he tumbled forward. Agent Lackey, only twenty-three years old, seated on the right side in the rear, was severely wounded by three bullets and slumped atop Smith, who had ducked forward when the firing began. Caffrey, standing beside Nash, whose body lay against the steering wheel, fell to the ground with a slug in his right temple. Hermanson and Grooms, nearest to the gunmen, slumped to the pavement together, Hermanson instantly killed when shot in the head, Grooms mortally wounded with a bullet in his side. Despite his grievous injury, Grooms managed to pull his pistol from a shoulder holster and get off two wild shots before succumbing. Vetterli, near the rear of the car and thereby partially protected from the screaming bullets, dropped to the ground. Miraculously, Smith was unscathed and Vetterli had only a single bullet crease on his arm.

Floyd, perhaps as startled as the officers by Miller's actions, never fired a shot during the wild episode.

"Come on, Verne, for Chris' sake," he suddenly yelled. "Let's get the hell outta here."

Miller began back-tracking toward the coupe as Floyd turned and ran, his back to the terrible carnage.

In front of the station, dozens of travelers, redcaps, and taxi drivers stood transfixed. Mrs. Lottie West, a caseworker for the Travelers Aid Society, was at her desk by the doorway when the first shots rang out. She noticed "a fat man"—Floyd, of course—and another white-shirted man near the site of the racket. A Kansas City Police Department motorcycle officer, Mike Fanning, was inside the station and ran to the doorway when he heard the shots.

"Shoot the fat man," Mrs. West yelled.

Fanning began firing with his service revolver at exactly the same time Vetterli arose to his feet, grabbed one of the rifles leaning against the death car, and aimed at the retreating Chevrolet. Through the rectangular back window of the fleeing car, he noticed "three figures" bent over in the coupe. What he actually saw was Miller, Floyd, and Miller's coat flung over the seat.

Vetterli and Fanning managed to hit the car's trunk four

times. Miller steered the car out of the parking lot, wheeled onto Pershing Road, then turned westward to Broadway. At Broadway, he sped south to Thirty-first Street, where he doubled back to the east. At the busy intersection of Thirty-first and Main, he roared through a red traffic light, observed by a streetcar operator, Robert D. Woods, who later told police he saw two men in a "new sedan, perhaps a Chevrolet," at 7:23 a.m. (Street cars usually ran on schedule in 1933, and Woods was to be at that junction at 7:23, which made the elapsed time correct if it was the killers' car he saw.)

"Where in the hell are you going?" Floyd wanted to know.

"Back to the house to get Richetti," replied Miller, who lived in a colonial-style home at 6612 Edgevale Road in Kansas City's South Side.

He was referring to Adam "Eddie" Richetti, who had been left at the house, ill from the effects of drinking the previous day and night. Floyd and Richetti had held up a bank in Mexico, Missouri, on June 14 and had zig-zagged across the state, trying to avoid the law. Within an hour of the robbery, Patrolman Ben Booth, aged thirty-eight, of the state highway patrol, and Sheriff Roger Wilson, forty-four, of Boone County, set up a roadblock near Columbia. Two men were halted, and while the officers were questioning them, one of the men drew a gun from under the seat and killed Booth. The sheriff grabbed one of the men, but the other killed him with another shot. Floyd and Richetti, identified as the robbers of the Mexico bank, were immediately tied to the twin shootings.

At dawn on June 16, their car began overheating and Richetti drove to his hometown of Bolivar, where his brother Joe worked in a garage. Their getaway car was steaming as the pair drove into Bitzer's Garage. Joe was on duty alone, and there was no one else around. The car's radiator was shot, so Floyd suggested they grab the first car to drive in. Unbelievably, Sheriff Jack Killingsworth was the first customer. His car was taken, and the desperadoes drove west out of town with the sheriff as hostage. Near Clinton, the pair halted a less conspicuous car and commandeered it, retaining the sheriff and the second car's driver as well. They detoured into Kansas, crossing the state line near Ottawa, where they spent the afternoon hiding in a brush-covered gulley. At dusk, they headed northeast, entering Kansas City near Lee's Summit, where they released the hostages. Realizing their normal haunts would be watched, they headed to "The White Horse," a gambling joint at Seventy-second and Troost, in Jackson County right at the city limits. Eddie Richetti, a heavy drinker, had been sipping homemade white lightning most of the day. He was heavily intoxicated when they arrived at the club. After gambling for a time, Floyd ran into Miller, who had heard radio reports about the search for the two Columbia killers. He suggested Floyd and Richetti spend the night at his home, since his wife was out of town. When they arrived at the Miller house, Richetti almost immediately passed out on a divan. Shortly after, the phone rang and Miller spent the next hour with a number of calls. He finally filled Floyd in.

"That was Doc Stacci in Chicago," he explained. "They nailed Frank Nash yesterday in Hot Springs and are bringing him here on the Little Rock Flyer. They want me to spring him when they take him off the train. Lazia has okayed it."

Stacci was a tavern owner in suburban Chicago who often acted as a go-between on shady deals. Dick Galatas, a Hot Springs gambler, had contacted Nash's wife, named a price to free her husband, and the wheels began to turn. Galatas called Stacci, who phoned Miller, who in turn had to get clearance from Johnny Lazia. No jewelry store could be robbed, no bank busted, no bookie joint raided without his okay. It was nearly dawn by the time the details were worked out. Miller felt he needed two more "guns" to do the job. Floyd, as Miller's guest, was obligated to go along;

the unknowing Richetti would be the third. They slept an hour, tried to rouse Richetti, but finally decided to do the job without him, figuring he'd be a handicap, anyhow.

Following the Union Station shooting, Miller felt Richetti should be awakened to flee with them.

"Christ, he's safe, nobody could put him at the scene," Floyd pointed out. "Let's get the hell outta town."

Miller acquiesced and steered the Chevrolet eastward on Highway 50 to Warrensburg, Missouri. There, Floyd stole a car and headed alone for Davis County, Iowa, where he knew a farmer who, for a substantial fee, hid men fleeing the law. He arrived at the farmer's house late on the night of June 17. He gave the farmer enough money to drive into a Ford agency in nearby Centerville, Appanoose County, the next morning and buy a new car.

Miller headed to Chicago, where he knew a bachelor named Raymond Walsh who made a living hiding getaway cars for criminals. In fact, Harvey Bailey, a notorious bank robber, had a Chrysler Imperial stored in Walsh's garage at the time. Miller arrived at Walsh's well after dark. When Walsh spotted the bullet holes in the back of the coupe, he was livid. He had heard about the massacre on the radio, and although none of the witnesses, including the three FBI agents who survived, identified Miller as one of the gunmen, Walsh immediately guessed Miller was involved.

"You crazy bastard, you'll get me hung," Walsh protested. "Get that damn car outta here."

Miller indicated he had no way to dispose of the car.

"I'll get rid of the Chevy," Walsh advised. "Take Bailey's car and I'll square up with him. Grab yourself a home brew out of the ice box and get going."

As Walsh got the coupe out of sight, Miller sat at the kitchen table drinking beer. When Walsh entered the house, he opened a bottle of beer and joined Miller at the table.

"What in the hell happened down in K.C. today, Verne?" Walsh asked.

Miller detailed the events, including the phone calls from Chicago, and explained how Chief Reed's shot, which killed Nash, ignited the entire shooting. Slowly, the hired killer got to his feet, thanked Walsh for his hospitality and the car exchange, and walked to the big Imperial Walsh had brought out.

"Tell Harvey I'll square up with him someday," he informed Walsh as he drove away, headed for New York. But Walsh knew he'd have to settle with Bailey, and wondered how soon the bank robber would show up. Bailey and ten other convicts had just escaped from the Kansas state prison and were thought to be hiding in the Cookson Hills of Oklahoma.

(Actually, it would be thirty-three years before Walsh and Bailey would see each other. In 1966, at a meeting in a Kansas City hotel room, Walsh revealed the story of the Union Station massacre to Bailey, as told to him by Miller. Tantalizingly, many aspects of the crime still remain unsolved mysteries. There is even some doubt, on the part of former members of the police department of Kansas City, Missouri, about who the gunmen were and whether they or the lawmen actually inflicted some of the fatal wounds. According to retired Maj. John Halvey, who later became chief of detectives of the force, "The mystery of Detective Hermanson's wounds was never even brought to the public's attention. I was one of the first patrolmen to arrive on the scene and the entire side of Hermanson's head had been blown off. Only a shotgun could have inflicted that type of wound. Chief Reed carried a shotgun [as well as a revolver] when escorting prisoners, and we wondered if in the shooting the gun had not accidentally been discharged [when Reed himself was shot in the head]. But the FBI covered up so many facts about the case, we never really knew much.")

The Union Station massacre became a turning point in American criminal history. The brazen slayings in broad daylight shocked the entire world and triggered a switch in the public's attitude. Since the stock market crash in 1929, many crimes in the United States had been against institutions, banks in particular. Soon it was apparent the country was falling in love with its bank robbers, a bizarre situation that historians and sociologists have never been able to explain. From early 1932 until the massacre, bank robbers were treated with respect normally reserved for royalty, their deeds broadcast daily and magnified by a news-hungry press seeking headlines to sell newspapers. Even those bank robbers who killed were excused by some, since it was usually "only a banker" who was murdered. But the awful slaughter at the Union Station jolted the public into a more realistic view of crime. It would require another full year for the love affair to burn out, but the passion was beginning to flicker.

The massacre also contributed to another period of significance in American crime. It marked the beginning of "the Hoover Era." J. Edgar Hoover, who had taken over the Bureau of Investigation (as it was then known) in 1924, struggled continually to keep it funded by Congress. He decided to use the killings as a springboard to bring attention to his bureau. A concentrated public-relations effort thrust Hoover into the limelight, and as his power increased, he capitalized on it by collecting dossiers on influential Americans. For the next four decades, Hoover's name struck fear in the hearts of criminals and public figures alike.

Many came to share the view of the vaunted king of bank robbers, Harvey Bailey, who often said: "That damn Hoover was a bigger crook than anybody at Alcatraz."

## The Love Affair

# 2

Early in 1932, an amazing phenomenon occurred in the United States. A wave of idolatry swept the depression-wracked nation, not unlike the hero worship enjoyed by the sports stars of the 1920s. Only this time the beneficiary was the common bank robber.

Chiefly responsible for this sudden "love affair" between the public and the bank robbers was the Great Depression that followed the stock market crash of 1929. Only three percent of America's workers had been unemployed in 1929. By 1932, the figure was almost twenty-four percent—twelve million people without jobs—and it was still increasing. In 1932, corn sold for only three cents a bushel, and despite promises of future improvement by the new president, Franklin Delano Roosevelt, conditions were bleak. The search for jobs drove hundreds of thousands of farm boys into the cities, and when many failed to find work, some resorted to crime to keep food in their stomachs. By the same token, city dwellers were often forced to steal to feed their families. It was this situation that helped spawn the unique romance of the unemployed workers and the impoverished farmers for the men who robbed the wealthy.

There were two other facets of life during the early days of the Great Depression that sped the situation along. Newspapers, perpetually seeking methods to increase street sales, found people liked to read about the derring-do of those who robbed banks for a living. Blazing headlines about the bandits of the day sold papers. Thus, reporters, vying with the opposition, created catchy nicknames for the new heroes, such as "Pretty Boy" Floyd, "Machine Gun" Kelly, "Baby Face" Nelson, while reporting their daily movements, however inaccurately. "Bonnie and Clyde," the killer team, were followed in the news columns as closely as "Mutt and Jeff," "Little Orphan Annie," and "Tarzan" in the comic sections. In the history of newspaper journalism in this country, reporters never developed more anti-heroes, concocted more outright fabrications, and titilated the public more than in the period from early 1932 until the crime picture changed in 1934. Even the well-publicized gangland days of Chicago and Al Capone in the late 1920s never received the treatment given the common bank robbers in those depression years.

A third factor was the lack of national heroes. In the 1920s, during "the golden age of sports," the public lavished its affection on sports figures. But by 1932, the mighty Babe Ruth was struggling in his last year as a New York Yankee, Bobby Jones had retired following his fantastic grand slam of golf in 1931, Jack Dempsey had been replaced by foreign fighters such as Primo Carnera and Max Schmeling in the world of heavyweight boxing, and Red Grange was winding down a brilliant football career. America needed new heroes. It was the combination of these bizarre conditions that thrust the common bank robber into the public's favor.

Vicariously, the people standing in the breadlines and eating in the soup kitchens rejoiced at the good fortune of those who struck it rich simply by taking from the wealthy bankers. The acceptance of bank robbing as a way of life increased as the depression deepened, and respect for the minions of law and order declined as a result. Not only did the millions of poor and idle Americans find someone to admire, they also found someone to hate—the banker, a symbol of greed and avarice. Anyone who had lost a home or farm by repossession applauded the bank losses. The act of robbery not only became excusable, it was laudatory in the minds of many.

There was a curious geographic concentration in the crime picture. More than seventy-five percent of the bank robberies committed in the early thirties were in the Midwest. The rest of the country had holdups, to be sure, but the bulk of the heists occurred in the wide-open spaces where there were few major highways and a great number of small-town banks. The states of Iowa, Missouri, Kansas, Texas, Oklahoma, Nebraska, and the Dakotas bore the brunt of the onslaught. (Illinois, Indiana, and Ohio would get theirs a bit later, in 1934 and '35, when the likes of Dillinger, Nelson, Homer Van Meter, and Harry Pierpont got together.)

Despite the peculiarity of geography, the entire nation joined in the craze. Idle people everywhere needed something exciting to think about. Daily papers from coast to coast and the weekly news magazines brought the deeds of the bank robbers to their eager readers.

Since midwestern America in the 1930s was mostly rural, dotted with thousands of small towns, it facilitated the art of bank robbing. The professionals liked the wide-open country, minimal security, and steady supply of targets the Midwest offered. The small towns usually had a bank, and most survived the crash of 1929. The loot was generally small compared to the large-city banks, but the lack of both traffic congestion and bank security in the small towns made them attractive targets. The pros sometimes challenged the large-city banks, but often shootings resulted. Seldom did anyone get shot in the small-town jobs.

In the minds of lawmen and his fellow bank robbers, Harvey Bailey in 1932 was the undisputed king of bank bandits. He had never been captured or charged, except for a minor clothing theft in 1920. He was credited with developing techniques in bank robbing that are used today. His meticulous planning was so detailed each person involved knew exactly what to do in any eventuality. In his twenty-nine known robberies, not a single bank official or customer was shot, although several were clubbed over the head when things didn't go according to plan. Only one of his fellow robbers was killed in the execution of a job, having been struck in the head by a wild bullet while they were fleeing.

Bailey's reputation was such that he was accused of practically every major haul in the Midwest from 1928 until his capture in 1932. He was credited with plotting the Lincoln, Nebraska, National Bank heist that netted more than two million dollars in 1930, and was even thought to have set up the robbery of the United States Mint in Denver, back in 1922. Both of these he vociferously denied, perhaps because there were shootings in each. His face was recognized by every law officer in the Midwest, yet he was never tied directly to any of the bank robberies he committed until his first accidental arrest in 1932.

Bailey could case a bank in a single visit. His memory was uncanny. With one look at a teller's cage, he could

mentally photograph the number of tills, any wires leading
to an alarm, or other pertinent information needed to complete a robbery in six to eight minutes. For him, proper
planning and execution included a fail-safe escape plan.
Bailey's utilization of country roads to avoid major-high-
way roadblocks was perhaps his greatest contribution to
the art. He perfected the method of "running the cat
roads." He would spend days driving on farm-to-market
roads surrounding an area where he planned a robbery. He
referred to these roads as cat roads because cats were about
the only ones who could use them after dark. Using a foot-
pedal odometer, he measured distances between points and
recorded them. A typical log might read:

"Drive 1.7 miles to schoolhouse on northeast corner of
intersection, turn right 7.9 miles to white farm house, turn
left 3.7 to intersection of JJ and N. Cross 53W and go 6
miles to next intersection."

The term "running the cat roads" became normal bank-
robber jargon. The technique was used successfully by the
majority of professionals. Only the amateurs—the desperate farm boy who was hungry, the city kid with no job, the
family man with no home for his children—were foolish
enough to stick up a bank without a plan. Many were
caught, and the state prisons were jammed as a result. This
created yet another sociological problem, as callow youths
were thrown together with hardened criminals in crowded
quarters.

An example of overcrowding was the Kansas State Penitentiary at Lansing. Eighteen hundred men were crammed
into cell houses built in 1865 and designed to hold nine
hundred inmates. The prisoners were fed in shifts, caf-
eteria style, in the overcrowded mess hall. Many worked on
the prison farm, which provided food for the convicts, the
guards and their families, and some state officials. Others
worked in the twine plant, which supplied the needs of

Kansas farmers. Still others were assigned to the coal mines, where whiskey stills and gambling flourished.

Other Midwest prisons were similarly bulging. At Mc-Alester, the Oklahoma State Penitentiary had more than double the normal complement of convicts, and Missouri's prison had hundreds of men confined in auxiliary sites.

The jammed conditions offered great escape possibilities for the old-timers behind walls. The overwhelming majority of inmates were strict newcomers to crime who gave little thought to escape. But to the old pros, it was a challenge, and they took full advantage of the undermanned guard posts, inefficient penal methods, political hacks appointed as wardens, and the live-and-let-live attitude resulting from the depressed economy. The numerous escapes made glaring headlines, and the reporters often invented stories to best the opposition. This not only boosted public interest, but further glorified the criminal.

Although the first signs of the public's love affair with bank robbers surfaced in 1932, it would be another year before the admiration peaked. John Dillinger was yet to make his first major bank robbery. When that deadly Indianan made the scene, a revival of interest in the deeds of bank robbers developed. But Dillinger and his cohorts were killers, and although national interest was intense, the love-affair aspects of the public's fascination dwindled.


In the first years of the depression, a typical attitude toward bank robbing was exemplified by the mother of a minor crook named George Magness. He and three friends robbed the only bank in the tiny Kansas town of Edna. Two days later they were captured near Stinnett, Texas, returned to their home county for trial. While in the Oswego, Kansas, jail, Magness was visited by various members of his family. When his mother saw her son behind bars, she became incensed and sought out Sheriff Al Coad.

Looking the law officer right in the eye, the irate mother began to berate him for incarcerating her son.

"Hell, sheriff," she concluded, "bank robbin' ain't hardly no crime at all."

# The Gangs

During the 1930s, the public's nodding approval of criminal gangs, as well as bank robbers, was another attitude that defied tradition. Historically, America never abided organized lawbreakers of any sort. Even Jesse and Frank James and their little band of train robbers were revered only by their Missouri neighbors, incensed at the railroads who took their lands for rights-of-way in the westward expansion. In the Old West, outlaws who banded together to loot and plunder, such as the infamous "Wild Bunch," were totally ostracized by the populace. Al Capone and his mob in Chicago, with more than a thousand gunmen, struck such fear in the hearts of the entire country that public pressure demanded their eradication. Gangs just were not popular with Americans.

Inexplicably, during the depression, two major gangs, along with a number of less potent ones, were accepted by the public, if not necessarily approved by them. In early

1933, the Barker-Karpis gang began to make headlines and reached its peak about the time of the Union Station massacre in June. Later, in 1934, John Dillinger's supergang became so awesome and well publicized that the public adopted them. Both gangs fouled their nests, literally, by leaving the bank robbing business and going into crimes against persons, including murder. Once this happened, criminals lost their glamor, and the forces of law and order once again moved to the fore with the public.

The Barker-Karpis outfit became the first big-time operation of the depression. Minor gangs led by such as Al Spencer, Jake Fleagle, and the Kimes brothers had been wiped out in the late twenties and early thirties but had never been as awesome as the Barker-Karpis combination. The Barrow brothers, accompanied by Clyde's girlfriend, Bonnie Parker, and a not-too-bright hanger-on named W. D. Jones, were never considered a gang in the true sense of the word. They were traveling companions who robbed, murdered, and stole cars at will, randomly. The Purple Gang of Detroit was more inclined toward bootlegging and faded away in the mid-thirties, but it too was loosely knit and didn't receive much publicity. Many other gangs controlled the rackets and resorted to non-headline crimes. The Barkers, Dock and Freddy, and their running mate, Alvin Karpis, went for the dramatic crimes. If they had stuck to bank robbing, history might have treated them more kindly, but two days before the Union Station massacre, they kidnapped a St. Paul brewing magnate. A stunned public, bombarded with news of violence and terror, began to lump bank robbers in with other criminals.

The Barker-Karpis gang got its start in the Kansas state prison, where Karpis and Freddy Barker were cellmates together. They decided to team up, and when they were released in 1931, they went to the Barker home in Tulsa. Fred's mother was living there with a ne'er-do-well alcoholic named Art Dunlop, her husband having given up

long ago on his wild family and returned to their former
home in Joplin, Missouri, where he worked as a filling-
station attendant. Together, Fred and Karpis began a series
of bungled crimes. They killed a sheriff in West Plains,
Missouri, and flubbed a couple of bank attempts. Arthur
"Dock" Barker, three years older than Fred, was a diminu-
tive five foot three, which possibly accounted for his mean-
ness in proving his manhood. From his youth in Webb
City, Missouri, where he was first arrested at the age of
eleven, until he wound up in the dreaded Alcatraz prison,
he was belligerent and violent. He was involved in at least
five killings during his crime career. While Freddy and
Karpis were the nucleus of the gang, Dock was in or out
depending on whether he liked the job being considered.
Of the other Barker boys, Lloyd was in Leavenworth on a
twenty-five-year stretch for robbing a post office. Herman
had been shot in a Newton, Kansas, battle with police and
either committed suicide when trapped (as the police reported) or was killed in the shoot-out.

As the youngest, Freddy was stuck with the job of caring
for his mother, a simple hillbilly woman from Aurora, Missouri, where all the boys had been born. Freddy hauled his
mother and Dunlop around the country with him. As the
gang's activities became more noteworthy, the FBI realized
that when they caught up with Barker, they'd probably
have to shoot the old woman, too. So Hoover had his crack
public-relations director, Courtney Ryley Cooper, issue re-
leases that "Ma" Barker, then past sixty, was the master-
mind behind the heists the gang pulled. This laughable
announcement obviously had no basis; the FBI had not
apprehended a single member of the gang nor anyone con-
nected with it in order to ascertain just who did the gang's
plotting. As Harvey Bailey noted years later: "The old
woman couldn't plan breakfast. When we'd sit down to
plan a bank job, she'd go in the other room and listen
to Amos and Andy or hillbilly music on the radio. She

just went along with Freddy because she had no choice. Freddy loved his mother and wouldn't leave her to fend for herself."

As for the gang, it had a floating membership. The most constant member was a three-quarter Cherokee Indian named Volney Davis, an old chum from Tulsa days. Others included Monty Bolton, Fred Goetz, Charley Fitzgerald, Larry DeVol, Bill Weaver, Harry Campbell, Frank Nash (who would be killed at the Union Station), Earl Christman, Jess Doyle, and James Wilson from time to time.

Another big gang was formed on Memorial Day, 1933, when eleven convicts went over the wall at the Kansas State Penitentiary. Harvey Bailey and Wilbur Underhill, a mentally disturbed cop-hater and four-time murderer, were the best known of the escapees, so the press immediately dubbed them "the Bailey-Underhill gang." Blazing headlines followed the chase, and every crime committed during the weeks that followed, including the Union Station massacre, was blamed on the fleeing felons.

Actually, the main group of escapees was composed of six men: Bailey, Underhill, Jim Clark, Bob Brady, Ed Davis, and Frank Sawyer. They were an incongruous bunch. Bailey was a sophisticate compared to the others and had lived in true luxury until his arrest. Underhill was a brutal and vicious psychotic, Brady was a country boy from Oklahoma who enjoyed his life of crime, Clark was a cunning and cool operator who couldn't find honest work to suit him, Davis was a small-timer who became a temperamental killer once he put a gun in his hand, and Sawyer was a taciturn Indian who had shot two men in gambling arguments. The other five, who joined the break uninvited, were diverse types—an Army deserter, a former chicken thief, an orphan on his own from the age of eleven, a car thief, and a drifter.

The press feverishly covered the day-by-day search for the fugitives, who had struck a chord with the public by the boldness of the daylight escape. People were fascinated by the radio reports and newspaper accounts of the chase. The weekly news magazines in America covered the story, and so did London newspapers, since Harvey Bailey had been a favorite of the British because of his sophisticated approach to his livelihood. The Bailey-Underhill mob was sharing headlines with the NRA, the WPA, the PWA, and the other bureaucratic efforts to ease the country out of the terrible depression.

The press bestowed joint leadership of the gang on Bailey and Underhill. The reporters, however, were not aware of the conflict between the main characters. Bailey despised Underhill's violent approach, and the semi-crazed Underhill resented Bailey's superior intellect and natural leadership. But Underhill respected the older man's talents as a bank robber and, in a showdown, always relented. The tension between the two never eased, but Bailey's word became law within the gang. As the protagonists wrestled for control, five law officers gave Bailey credit for saving their lives when the crazed Underhill wanted to kill them, following the Memorial Day prison break. What quirk of fate determined that the sophisticated Chicago business-man turned bank robber and the Joplin, Missouri, killer would wind up buried within a half-mile of each other?

## The Golfers

Harvey John Bailey stood in the doorway of the Haven Hill apartments in Kansas City's exclusive Country Club Plaza. After carefully surveying Forty-seventh Street, which ran in front of the building, he swung a canvas golf bag over his right shoulder and strode quickly to a parked green Plymouth coupe at curbside. He inserted a key in the car door lock and stepped back as a rush of hot air swept past the opened door. He flung the golf bag with its wooden-shafted handmade clubs onto the ledge behind the coupe's seat, then eased his six-foot one-inch frame behind the wheel.

It was July 8, 1932, and like many summer mornings in Kansas City, it was muggy hot. The clock in the Plaza office building indicated it was almost 9 a.m. as Bailey pulled the coupe into the slow-moving traffic along the street. At Pennsylvania Street, he steered south to Ward Parkway where he doubled back eastward. Moments later, in front

of the Lucarno Apartments at 239 Ward Parkway, he
braked the coupe to a stop. Another man attired in golf togs
impatiently jerked open the coupe door:

"Where in the hell have you been, Harve? It's hotter
than hell out here," the man said.

Bailey geared the car into the traffic before he answered.

"Take it easy, Tommie. We'll be on the course in an
hour if that damn fence sold those bonds." He was referring to some Liberty bonds taken from the Citizen's National Bank of Fort Scott, Kansas, just three weeks before,
on June 17. Bailey, Tommie Holden (the other golfer in the
coupe), Red Phillips, Alvin Karpis, Freddy Barker, and
Larry DeVol had robbed the bank of $32,000 in cash and
negotiable bonds. A fence named Jack McBride was attempting to sell the bonds allotted to Bailey, Holden, and
DeVol. A meeting with him had been set prior to the golf
game.

"That damn fence is a real bastard," Holden mumbled,
never taking his eyes from the street. For some time, he
had the feeling he was being trailed. He and Francis Keating (known as the "Evergreen bandits" after they had held
up a train in a Chicago suburb, Evergreen Park, in 1928)
had simply walked out of the federal penitentiary at Leavenworth, Kansas, in 1931 following sentencing on the train
heist. The pair had escaped with the help of a young bootlegger named George Barnes. Barnes was working in the
prison's Bertillon room, where records and photos were
kept, and he had provided them with forged passes that
they used on a new guard. The embarrassed prison officials
had placed a priority on recapture of the pair.

Holden and Keating fled to Kansas City, then to St. Paul,
and, aided by the proceeds from several small bank robberies, managed to elude the FBI agents hot on their trail
for a year. But Holden had the eerie sense of being followed
everywhere he and his wife moved. Back in Kansas City,
they moved into the elite Lucarno, and the Keatings set up

residence on the same street at 722 Ward Parkway in the James Russell Lowell apartments. Like Bailey, Holden and Keating loved to play golf and used expensive handmade clubs manufactured by the Kenneth Smith Company, which had offices in Kansas City. While Holden, Bailey, and DeVol were taking care of the Fort Scott bank bond business, Keating was en route to the Kenneth Smith shop at Seventeenth and Broadway to pick up some repaired clubs prior to meeting the others at the Old Mission golf course. It was one of the public courses that permitted local ethnic groups and others who weren't in the country-club set to play. The course was almost within walking distance of the Country Club Plaza, located just west of the state line on the Kansas side. The half-dozen private courses elected not to allow Jews, Italians, or blacks to play, and the Old Mission course was popular, as a result, with the Italian residents of Kansas City's North End, including Johnny Lazia, the city's crime boss. When Frank Nash, for example, visited Kansas City he could often be found at the Old Mission course with Bailey and his friends. Although Freddy Barker and Alvin Karpis didn't play the game, they often met associates in the clubhouse. It was truly an outlaw hangout.

As Bailey approached the busy downtown area, he began searching for a parking place near the lawyer's office where the meeting about the bonds was to be held. In front of a large department store, Emery, Bird & Thayer, he found an open slot. The shiny new Plymouth, which Bailey called his "git" car because it was fast, easily slid into the parking area. The men hurried to a nearby office building, took an elevator to the fourth floor, and entered the attorney's office. McBride and his partner, a shady character named Johnny French, were waiting. French extracted several manila envelopes from a valise and tossed them on a desk in front of Bailey.

"There she is, boys. There's twenty-one $100 bills, the

best we could get for them bonds these days. Times is tough," French stated. "In fact, there's one $500 bond in DeVol's batch we couldn't move at all. Somebody want to take it to him?"

DeVol, who was supposed to be present for the swag split, didn't show up.

Holden wasn't happy with the fences' efforts. "Look, you bastards, that's not near enough for them bonds. We should have at least another grand," Holden yelled at them.

Bailey had experience dealing with hot bonds and money, having handled the $200,000 some friends got in the 1922 Denver mint robbery and the more than $2 million others took from the Lincoln, Nebraska, bank in 1930. He tried to calm Holden.

"Tommie, in this damn depression even Liberty bonds aren't moving," the older bandit said. "Let's go."

Bailey picked up DeVol's envelope and stuffed it in the hip pocket of his golf knickers. He put his share in with it. Holden was still fuming when the pair returned to the car and headed for the course.

Meanwhile, Keating had picked up his clubs at the golf plant. Trailing less than a block away was Agent Caffrey of the FBI (one of the men who would be killed less than a year later at Union Station). He had been shadowing Keating and Holden for more than four months. About the time he'd get set to recapture the bandits, they'd move to another town. In Kansas City, Caffrey picked up their trail by watching the golf course. He had spotted Keating and learned where he lived, following him to his Ward Parkway apartment.

At Forty-seventh and State Line, Keating turned into the Old Mission drive. He spotted Bailey's green Plymouth in the parking lot. In the clubhouse, Bailey and Holden were visiting with Freddy Barker. When Keating arrived at the table, Bailey explained that DeVol had not shown up at the meeting with the fences.

"Let's get out there before it's too damn hot," the anxious Holden said. Barker arose and indicated he was going to meet his buddy, Karpis, at their apartment in the Villa Carmen, 414 West Forty-sixth Terrace, which was a block from Bailey's Haven Hill residence.

"Tell your ma hello," Bailey yelled at Barker. Ma Barker would be home listening to the radio, as usual.

Holden, Bailey, and Keating made their way to the locker room.

In the parking lot, Caffrey watched closely from his Ford as the three golfers left the clubhouse for the course. Certain they would be there for a time, he drove to the Plaza to call the Kansas City, Missouri, police department. Since so many men in the department were corrupt and on the underground payroll of Johnny Lazia, Caffrey had to be careful. He realized Holden and Keating had contacts on the force, as did every major crime figure in the area.

"Let me talk to Tom Higgins," he told the department dispatcher. Higgins was the captain of detectives.

"Hello, Tom, this is Caffrey. You know those boys I was telling you about? They're ready. Can you get some officers and meet me at the Old Mission golf club?"

Higgins, noting Caffrey chose not to mention the escapees by name, assured the agent he'd have some men there within the hour.

Caffrey replaced the earpiece in the cradle and returned to his car. Back in the club parking lot, he waited impatiently for Higgins. The detective chief arrived with Officers Charles Little and Charles Costello of Kansas City, Kansas, and Harry Reed, Prime McDonough, and "Doc" Thurman of Kansas City, Missouri—all hand-picked, honest policemen. The agent led them to the pro shop, where the club professional, Bill Wotherspoon, greeted Caffrey.

"Hi. Are you still looking for somebody?"

Caffrey had stopped several times to ask Wotherspoon if he'd seen Frank Nash, another federal escapee, around the club. Nash's prison picture showed him to be bald, but he wore a wig and Wotherspoon had failed to recognize him, although the bank and train robber had played there many times.

Caffrey told the pro he was looking for someone else this time. He flashed pictures of Holden and Keating. The pro instantly recognized them.

"Hey, these guys are out on the course right now. Ought to be coming up on Number Eight pretty soon," Wotherspoon indicated.

Caffrey thanked the pro and led his troops outside.

"See that clump of trees down there," Caffrey said, pointing to a knot of scrub oaks about two hundred yards from the clubhouse. "Let's go down there and head them off before somebody around here gets an idea about warning them."

A dry gulley ran into the cluster of trees, which allowed the officers to hide easily. Soon they heard a thud as a golf ball landed on the green less than twenty yards away, followed by two more balls striking the ground. Oddly enough, Caffrey allowed the three men to putt out before stepping from his hiding place.

"Hold it, boys," Caffrey shouted.

The three golfers turned and stared. Bailey demanded to know what in the hell was going on.

Caffrey looked straight at Holden.

"Tommie, the jig is up. You'll be back in Leavenworth tomorrow morning."

Protesting innocence all the way, Holden and Keating were herded back to the clubhouse. Bailey was told to come along too, although Caffrey had no idea who he was. In the parking lot, all three men were thoroughly searched. When the manila envelope was pulled from Bailey's hip pocket, his heart froze. "That damned Liberty bond," he thought. The agent examined the bond carefully.

"What's your name, mister?"

"John Brown. I live at Seven Hundred West Forty-seventh."

"Where in the hell did you get this bond?"

"It belongs to another fella. I just picked it up for him," which was the truth.

"You better come on down to headquarters while we check this out," Captain Higgins decided. "And I also want to know what a gent like you is doing with twelve hundred bucks in your pocket." Not only the bond but the large amount of cash, particularly large for depression times, had aroused the officer's suspicions.

Once again fate worked against the captives. At the moment they were being queried by the officers, a snazzy Buick sportster roared into the parking lot. Behind the wheel was Lillian Holden, thirty, and her passengers, Marjorie Keating, twenty-six, and Mary Phillips, the wife of Red Phillips. Caffrey recognized the wives of Holden and Keating and ordered the car halted. The women, seeing their husbands manacled, ran toward them. The other woman remained seated in the car. She later told officers she was Mary Crawford and was visiting the Holdens.

A search of the car produced a suitcase containing two automatic pistols and seventy dollars in gold. The women joined their husbands on the trip to the station. "Mary Crawford" was released.

At the station, Holden and Keating admitted their identity. They signed over their property, including the golf bags, to their wives, who were then released. By dawn, the escapees were en route to Leavenworth. Police, incidentally, never learned the true identity of "Mary Crawford."

Later, officers searched the Holden apartment and found an expensive wardrobe, ammunition, and some cash. At Keating's place, it was the same. In Bailey's apartment, it was discovered "John Brown" had fifteen suits, a dozen sports coats, ammunition, and a Luger automatic pistol that fired ten shots from a cannister magazine much like a submachine gun. One officer recalled that a witness to the Fort Scott holdup reported seeing such a weapon in the hands of one of the robbers. When officers totaled the loot in the three apartments, they came up with more than seven thousand dollars in cash plus hundreds of rounds of ammunition and several weapons. The Keating car and the Buick sportster were confiscated, but officers overlooked Bailey's green coupe in the Old Mission parking lot. The next day, a friend of Bailey's drove the car from the lot, smashed it in a collision with another automobile, and fled the scene. Records showed the disabled vehicle was registered to John Brown.

In the meantime, the police were having the Liberty bond traced. They soon learned it had been stolen from the Fort Scott bank.

Still unaware of his identity, the police believed that "John Brown" was really "John J. Brennan," another alias Bailey often used. But an unexpected source led them to the truth.

Bailey had called for a Minneapolis lawyer, and when he arrived, Bailey was allowed to talk to him near the booking desk. A farmer from Sullivan County, Missouri, where the Bailey farm was located, was in the station on a speeding charge. He spotted Bailey talking to the lawyer.

"Say," the old farmer said, "you must be Harvey Bailey. You look just like your sister."

Bailey, cool as ever, turned to the old man.

"I don't recall ever meeting you, sir."

"You haven't. I live near your mother and sister up near Green City. I seen you when you come up to visit them when they caught that 'Killer' fellow."

Bailey knew he'd been "made."

The incident the farmer referred to involved Fred

"Killer" Burke, a machine gunner in the St. Valentine's Day massacre in Chicago, who was discovered on a farm next to the one owned by Bailey. The gunman had been a guest in the Bailey home in January, 1931, after Bailey, a former Chicagoan, had a request from the Capone gang to help hide Burke. Introduced as "Fred White," Burke became part of the community and married the daughter of a neighboring farmer. Mrs. Amanda Bailey, totally ignorant of Burke's background, thought her son's friend was a nice real-estate man from Chicago until a Green City, Missouri, service-station operator saw Burke's picture in *True Detective* magazine. The sheriff nailed Burke in his father-in-law's farm home. Bailey was called from Kansas City to explain his tie with the mobster, who was taken to Michigan to stand trial for the murder of a state patrolman.

The identification of Bailey and his possession of the stolen bond galvanized the police into action. Bailey was whisked to Fort Scott to stand trial for robbing the bank. Almost beyond belief, just days before, three Oklahoma prison escapees had been sentenced to life for that same crime. Jim Clark, Ed Davis, and Frank Sawyer had been picked up by Nevada, Missouri, sheriff's officers on June 17 and turned over to Fort Scott authorities, who charged them with the bank job. They were convicted, and the day before Bailey was picked up in Kansas City playing golf, the judge sentenced the three men, innocent of that charge, to life imprisonment as habitual criminals. When Bailey came to trial, he could not reveal the innocence of the others without implicating himself. Found guilty, he was sentenced, as a first offender, to a lesser term, ten to fifty years, further compounding the miscarriage of justice. Bailey joined the others in the Kansas state prison in August, 1932, shortly before his forty-sixth birthday.

Bailey adjusted quickly to the prison routine, eased by his ability to purchase things at the "Chouteau store," a prison facility for inmates to buy candy, toothpaste, and extras not provided routinely. His niece in Kansas City sent him money via a cook in the prison kitchen when supplies were brought in. This convenience would later be instrumental in the great Memorial Day prison break.

Bailey's outside contacts also assured him a "fix" was on in the state capital that would have him freed within a year. He settled down to the prison life at Lansing, comfortable in the knowledge he was soon to be sprung.

Behind the walls, the elder statesman ran into several acquaintances from his early crime days, which began following World War I. After serving as a railroad fireman from 1905 until drafted into the army in 1918, Bailey saved enough money to maintain the family farm in Sullivan County, Missouri, get married, and have two sons. When veterans who had been called up earlier returned to the railroad after the Armistice was signed, he was kept on, but only for occasional extra work. By the time Prohibition arrived in 1920, Bailey was ready to try something else to support his family. He bought the warehoused liquor belonging to John Pendergast, brother of Tom Pendergast, the political boss of Kansas City, and began running it illegally to Tulsa, St. Joseph, and Council Bluffs, Iowa. He became downright wealthy overnight. He drove a huge black Buick in his runs and because of this got into his first brush with the law. The Buick was not only fast, but could hold a good deal of material in the trunk and back seat. So, when several confederates located a clothing store in Maryville, Missouri, that carried expensive clothes, they cut Bailey in for a piece of the action if he'd let them use his car. Not only did they bungle the job and get caught, but Bailey's ownership of the vehicle was discovered. He posted $2,000 bond but chose not to show up for the trial and forfeited the bond and the car. He never again let anyone use one of his cars, except unknowingly many years later following the Union Station massacre.

After the Maryville experience, he thought safe-cracking

might be a better way to make a living. He joined with a number of others of the same mind, and they hit a dozen small-town banks in Iowa and North Dakota at night. The take wasn't worth the risk, he determined, and decided to go straight again. He moved his family to Ottumwa, Iowa, where he farmed and opened a bank account in the Ottumwa Savings Bank under the name of "Tom Brennan."

Bailey's agricultural career soon ended when he and three others, Nick "Chaw Jimmie" Traynor, "Dude" Richardson, and Alvin Johnston, robbed a bank on Euclid Avenue in Des Moines, netting $12,000. It whetted Bailey's appetite for the big time. On September 28, 1922, they all joined with Jimmie "Wolf" Lindon and Curly Santle to hit the Hamilton County Bank of Cincinnati. The loot in cash and negotiable bonds was finally assessed at $265,000.

Bailey and his friends then began casing a bank in Denver. When they were about ready to make their move, Bailey was notified his brother Jim was desperately ill with a brain tumor in Detroit. Bailey left the gang to be with his ailing brother and remained twenty-eight days. During that time, he read that the Denver mint had been robbed of $200,000 in cash in an amazing daylight holdup. A guard had been killed and probably one of the four bandits. A second holdup man was thought to have been wounded as well. Bailey, who always avoided government holdups because "they'll spend a million to recover a penny," wondered what prompted his erstwhile cohorts to change from the bank to the mint. A few weeks later Johnston contacted him to help sell the hot money from the mint.

After helping dump the money, Bailey moved his family to the Chicago area. He lived in Maywood, had an account in the Burns Bank in Cicero, later found a home in Calumet City. With some $85,000 in cash stashed in a safe-deposit box, Bailey decided to go straight again. He and a partner started two Standard Oil service stations, one in Calumet City and another in Hammond, Indiana, on heavily traveled thoroughfares next to railroad sidings, so tank-car lots could be purchased. The bulk purchases allowed the station to sell gasoline two cents cheaper, a strategy later followed by many operators. The partners then developed the first conveyor system for washing and polishing cars, also used widely today. The boys made Dun and Bradstreet.

Despite the perpetual battle to stay ahead of the competition through innovations and promotions, Bailey became restless with the life of a service-station operator. He spent considerable time at Capone speakeasies and "scatters" (pool halls or taverns) and soon got to know Capone and his associates on a first-name basis. Capone tried to convince Bailey to quit stealing and join the mob.

"Al, you got too many stoolies working for you," Bailey told the gangland chief. "One of them would someday rat on me and I'd have to put a bullet through his head."

Capone employed hundreds of men with the sole task of checking the gambling, prostitution, and bootlegging operations. If an employee in a speakeasy was caught or even suspected of holding out or skimming, he was beaten or killed by the enforcers in the gang. Few workers had the courage to try anything on "Big Al."

Bailey remained straight during his tenure as a service-station owner except for one time in the summer of 1925 when he joined a group "just for the hell of it." Eddie Fitzgerald was the son of a Kansas construction company owner who was put to work by his father following graduation from Kansas University. The young man had no interest in the construction business and one day pocketed the firm's payroll and took off. He got into bank robbing for a living and admired Bailey's reputation as a planner. He attempted to lure Bailey back into action.

"We've got this little town down in Kansas that's a cinch," Fitzgerald indicated. Bailey decided to go along as a fill-in, but when he saw the tiny bank, he told the group it was hardly worth the risk.

"The town was so small I can't remember its name, but it was in south central Kansas someplace," Bailey recollected. "We got about four thousand dollars and I think my share was about nine hundred. It was a long drive for that kind of money."

Bailey resisted other efforts until 1926, when Fitzgerald, Bailey's old companion Al Johnston, and a pro named "Slim" Jones got together and invited Bailey to do the casing and run the cat roads on a job in LaPorte, Indiana. The excitement of the project swept Bailey back into the business of bank robbing. The gang, along with two Peoria, Illinois, pickup bandits, took the LaPorte bank for $140,000 on November 12, 1926. Less than three weeks later, Bailey, Fitzgerald, Jones, Johnston, and Larry DeVol knocked off the Olmsted County Bank & Trust in Rochester, Minnesota, for $30,000. The gang was really clicking and struck again on August 19, 1927, ripping off the Farmer's National Bank of Vinton, Iowa, for seventy grand. On February 6, 1928, they took the People's and Drovers Bank of Washington Court House, Ohio, for $225,000 in bonds and cash.

Fitzgerald heard about a possibility in Washington, Iowa, but after running the cat roads, Bailey was convinced the escape route was too touchy. They settled on the Whitney Loan & Trust of Atlantic City, Iowa, instead. The group this time included a giant of a man, Homer Wilson, who had known Bailey from his safe-cracking days. They divided $55,000 in cash and Liberty bonds.

Flushed with success, Bailey and his boys hit the Sturgis, Minnesota, bank for $80,000 on December 18, 1928, and rocked the bank in Clinton, Indiana, for $52,000 just before Christmas. Bailey spent the holidays with his mother and sister on the family farm in Missouri before returning to the Chicago area.

Bailey took stock of his string of successes. He and various associates had looted nearly $1 million in cash and bonds. Bailey's shares, ranging from a fifth to a seventh

depending on the size of the crew, netted him around
$100,000, since the hot bonds were fenced for considerably
less than face value. Of that he had $85,000 in cash in a
safe deposit box in Calumet City.

The ease with which banks were robbed took a lot of the
challenge out of the life for Bailey. He once again decided
to go straight and return to the operation of the service
stations. After a few weeks back in the routine, it was apparent he and his partner had to sell the stations and get
into something more exciting.

Bailey took his share of the proceeds and much of the
$85,000 in bank-robbing loot and put the total to work
drawing interest. He opened a bank account. Again, the
man who had stolen more than a million dollars in assets
from similar institutions entrusted his fortune to a bank.

Bailey's lust for excitement and challenge continued
after the sale of the service stations. When some buddies
suggested the First National Bank of Cherokee, Iowa, had
been cased and looked like an easy mark, he joined in the
raid. Later in the summer, he joined his cohorts in taking
the Emmet County State Bank in Estherville, Iowa. Bailey
cased the bank and ran the cat roads. On August 29, 1929,
he walked through the bank door and demanded cashier
Wayne Currell hand over the money. The bank's contribution was less than $2,000, but customer M. K. Whelan pro-
vided $3,350 in negotiable bonds he had in his hand when
Bailey and friends walked in. Outside, the driver and another bandit terrorized the people on the street with a shotgun and machine gun. A fifteen-year-old boy managed to
phone for help, but by the time law enforcement officers
arrived, the bandits were gone.

Two months later, the world was stunned on that black
October Friday by the market crash. Bailey was virtually
wiped out. The bank that held his savings was one of the
thousands around the nation that failed. His real-estate
holdings were depleted and all he had left was part of the

original $85,000 in cash he kept in a safe-deposit box. For all practical purposes, Harvey Bailey was broke.

He returned to the farm life of his youth and bought a dairy farm in Kenosha County, Wisconsin. He and his wife and two sons attempted to develop a dairy business, and with times so tough, the operation never got off the ground. He decided to return to the business he knew best, bank robbing.

Meanwhile, Tommie Holden and Francis Keating had walked away from the penitentiary at Leavenworth. They headed for St. Paul, a "protected" city much like Hot Springs, Arkansas, controlled by gamblers, and Kansas City, under the thumb of Tom Pendergast. The Evergreen bandits owed a debt to the young bootlegger who helped fake their passes that allowed them to get past a guard, and when Barnes, now known as Kelly, was released he followed the pair to St. Paul. As part of the returned favor, they let him in on a job they were planning on the bank of Willmar, Minnesota. Thus Machine Gun Kelly was about to rob his first bank.

In addition to Bailey, Holden, and Kelly, three minor characters were added, one known as "Jew Sammy" Stein. On July 15, 1930, the gang hit the bank. It wasn't a smooth operation and shooting broke out. As the bandits fled with $70,000, a random bullet caught Stein in the back of the head. Somewhere east of Rochester, Minnesota, the robbers hid the body in some underbrush.

Two months later, Bailey rounded up a new gang to make a personal call on the Ottumwa, Iowa, Savings Bank in the town where he once lived. For this one he got Freddy Barker, Howard Phillips, Holden, and former South Dakota sheriff turned bank robber, Verne Miller. They took the bank without a hitch and Bailey got back some of the money he'd lost in the crash. The robbery occurred September 9, 1930.

On September 17, one of the largest hauls in bank-rob-

bing history occurred in Lincoln, Nebraska. Eddie Fitzgerald led the band that took $2,654,700 in negotiable
securities and $24,000 in cash from the Lincoln National
Bank. The bank went broke. Word was flashed that the
execution was so smooth, surely Harvey Bailey had master-
minded it. Although Bailey was in Minneapolis at the time
of the heist, the FBI was certain he had taken part in the
unbelievable daylight robbery. Oddly, Fitzgerald rushed to
Minneapolis with the hot securities to solicit Bailey's help
in unloading them. Bailey went to Gus Winkler, a notorious arranger for the Capone mob, known otherwise as the
Syndicate, who managed to sell most of the paper. In the
ensuing months, the hot bonds showed up all over the
country, selling for as little as fifty cents on the dollar.

Solvent again, Bailey became more selective in his jobs.
He called a meeting in Kansas City to discuss a Texas project, the Sherman Central State Bank. The group that met
on March 15, 1931, in his room at the Hotel President
included Verne Miller, now a Kansas City resident, whose
criminal activities went unsuspected and who played golf
with the country-club set. After the meeting, Miller ran
into George Kelly and his red-haired bride, Kathryn, on the
street in front of the hotel. Kelly, having gone through his
$12,000 share of the Willmar, Minnesota, job, hit Miller
for a loan. Miller suggested he go upstairs and try Bailey,
who was registered under the name of "Thompson," but
warned Kelly to leave his wife outside.

"You know how Harve hates having women around,"
Miller reminded. Bailey refused to allow wives or sweet-
hearts to be in on the planning or execution of any robbery,
feeling there was more possibility of mishaps.

Kelly went to Bailey's room and applied the touch. Bailey
peeled out $1,000 and handed it to the pudgy-faced ex-
salesman turned bootlegger and part-time bank robber.

"I don't know when I can pay you back, Harve, but I
will," said the man who would one day be rated number
one on the FBI's most-wanted list.

Bailey decided to let Kelly in on the proposed Sherman heist. They made plans to meet in Dallas. When the group assembled in Dallas, it was decided that Bailey, Miller, Frank Nash, and a hood called Dutch Joe, who had been with the gang at Willmar, would hit the bank and that Kelly would meet them near the Louisiana line with a second getaway car. The bank produced $40,000. When they met, three of the bandits joined Kelly in his car. Bailey and Dutch Joe continued on together. The group reassembled in Hot Springs, Arkansas, and quickly split the loot, Kelly failing to remember his loan from Bailey five weeks earlier.

Bailey and Dutch Joe drove back to Kansas City, then to Chicago, where Bailey stashed his big Chrysler Imperial at the residence of Ray Walsh. He would leave the car stored there until he needed it, perhaps as long as a year later. In case anyone had spotted it in the Sherman robbery, it would be "cooled" by the time he drove it again.

Bailey returned to Kansas City and, with his wife, moved into the classy Haven Hill apartment in the Plaza. Holden, Keating, Freddy Barker and Alvin Karpis, Larry DeVol, and Frank Nash maintained apartments within a mile of each other in the Plaza area. In another part of the city, a young man from Oklahoma's Cookson Hills was garnering a reputation as a tough guy with a pleasing, friendly countenance. They called him "Pretty Boy," but not to his face.

On June 17, 1932, Bailey, Karpis, Holden, Barker, DeVol, and Phillips relieved the Fort Scott, Kansas, bank of $32,000. They returned to Kansas City, divided the loot, and returned to the life of luxury.

The next morning, the Kansas City *Times* reported that three men had been picked up near Nevada, Missouri, and identified as the robbers of the Fort Scott bank. In Kansas City, the actual bandits were getting out their golf sticks.

## The Innocent Thieves

The black Buick sedan came to a stop directly in front of the Rich Hill, Missouri, State Bank. Two men wearing bib overalls stepped from the car and briskly strode toward the bank doors. A third man remained behind the wheel of the idling car. Suddenly, one of the men slowed his pace, then stopped, as the other continued on, swinging open the screen door, sending a swarm of flies buzzing into the air. Realizing he was alone, the man in the lead, short and wiry with red hair, looked back at his companion and instantly realized he had frozen in fear. The leader spun on his heel, grabbed the dazed man by the arm, and shoved him back into the Buick. The driver ground the gears and roared away. Dust, marking a trail, billowed behind the speeding car.

"I ought to kill you right now, you son of a bitch," the driver growled, glancing toward his reluctant cohort.

"Take it easy, Ed," the red-haired man advised. "Let's get the hell outta here and come back tomorrow." The

Buick continued to raise huge clouds of dust as it reached Highway 71, where the driver headed south at a high rate of speed.

It was June 17, 1932, and the tiny coal-mining town of Rich Hill almost had its only bank robbed. Unbeknown to the three would-be bandits, at the very same moment six men were successfully robbing the First National Bank of Fort Scott, Kansas, about fifty miles away.

Jim Clark, Ed Davis, and Frank Sawyer had chosen the Rich Hill bank because they felt it was so small it didn't require casing. With less than a dollar between them, they were hungry and the Buick was running low on fuel. The bank appeared to be a solution to their problem.

The three men were escapees from the Oklahoma state prison at McAlester, but on different breaks. Clark had walked away from a prison road-camp near the community of Colby the previous April 25. Davis had escaped from the main institution at McAlester only two weeks before. Sawyer, like Davis a convicted murderer serving life, had been out since 1930 when he fled a work detail.

The trio got together chiefly because of a half-breed Indian named Marion Pike, who had a cabin deep in the rugged Cookson Hills country of northeast Oklahoma. Clark went directly to Pike's cabin following his escape. Davis had gone to the home of another Cherokee, Charles Dotson, in Oklahoma City. One day, Davis and Dotson, who had relatives in the Cooksons, arrived at Pike's cabin. Clark and Davis compared notes. Several days later, they met again, this time at Dotson's place. Sawyer was a friend of Dotson's and happened by while Clark and Davis were there. The three escapees decided they needed money and a good car. They set out together to obtain both.

With Clark behind the wheel of an old car of Sawyer's, they drove west out of Oklahoma City to the town of Yukon. They spotted two women employees of the Oklahoma Gas & Electric Company going to El Reno for a company picnic. Clark pulled alongside the women's auto and

Sawyer jumped on the running board. The trio relieved the women of their watches, diamond rings, and black Buick. They then headed for Missouri to find a bank to rob. The next day they found Rich Hill.

Davis, thirty-two, possessed a trigger temper that was accented with a gun in his hand. In trouble since the age of nineteen, he seldom raised his voice but everyone knew not to rile him. He was still fuming when he pulled the Buick onto a side road near Nevada, Missouri, following the Rich Hill incident.

"Sawyer, what in the hell happened there? How come you froze like that?"

Sawyer, a three-quarter Cherokee Indian, glared in silence at the driver from the back seat of the sedan. A gambler who had killed two men in separate arguments while playing cards, Sawyer was the only one of the three with previous bank-robbing experience. He offered no ready explanation why he suddenly panicked.

Clark tried to soothe Davis by suggesting they rest a while to cool off. Sawyer swung open the back doors of the car and stretched out. Beside him were two rifles, a Colt .45 revolver, and a sawed-off shotgun covered with the cutoff leg of a pair of overalls. In the front seat, Davis and Clark each had automatic pistols beside them.

Clark unfolded a Conoco road map and began tracing the cat roads in the Rich Hill vicinity. As Sawyer dozed in the back, Clark and Davis became engrossed in the map and didn't notice a car turning onto the side road from the highway. The sound of a horn startled the trio and Clark swung around to see a farmer sitting in a Ford, unable to get by the opened rear door of the Buick. Sawyer swung the door shut, and all three waved at the driver as he eased past. Three miles down the road, the farmer stopped at his sister's house to phone Sheriff W. E. Butner at Nevada, Missouri.

"Sheriff, this is Walt Sands. I just passed three tough-looking birds in a big car with Oklahoma plates parked east

of my sister's house. You know the L. H. Myers place
northeast of town? Well, they're parked just off 71 there,"
the farmer reported.

The sheriff reacted quickly. Bulletins about the Fort
Scott robbery had alerted law officers in Missouri, Kansas,
and Oklahoma. Nevada was only twenty-three miles from
Fort Scott and Sheriff Butner instantly thought of the bank
bandits.

Accompanied by his young son Stan and two deputies,
Woody Stanum and Ade Tae, Sheriff Butner rushed to the
Myers farm. They spotted the Buick parked beneath a huge
elm tree. Before the occupants knew what was happening,
they were surrounded and the armament was discovered. A
coat in the car bore the label of the McEwen-Halliburton
Clothing Company of Oklahoma City, and the car seemed
to fit the description of "a black and dark-green Buick with
Oklahoma plates" used in the Fort Scott robbery. Although
he was puzzled when no money was found in the car, Sheriff Butner was sure he had captured part of the gang that
robbed the bank.

The prisoners were put in the Nevada jail where they
gave their names as George Allen of "anywhere," Jack
Martin, Peggs, Oklahoma, and Bob Morgan, Cleveland,
Ohio.

The next morning a large crowd gathered around the
Vernon County jail. Reports of the capture attracted considerable attention, and when bank officials and other witnesses from Fort Scott arrived to identify the culprits,
several hundred people were on hand. Butner went back to
search the area for hidden loot after officers took the captives to Fort Scott to stand trial. Each had been solidly
identified as one who robbed the Kansas bank.

Despite their pleas of innocence and their claims they
were trying to rob the Rich Hill bank while the Fort Scott
job was being pulled, the three escapees were arraigned,
tried, and found guilty. They were sentenced to life im-

prisonment on July 7, the day before Harvey Bailey was picked up in Kansas City. Four days later, Bailey was taken to Fort Scott for trial. He was convicted and joined them in Lansing a few weeks later.

Of the three "innocents," Clark was the most bitter. He immediately set about devising an escape plan. Prison testing indicated he had an I.Q. of 98 and a grade level of 4.7. His farm background was the basis for his job assignment, caring for the mules that hauled the heavy coal cars in the mines. The job permitted him adequate time to plot a break.

Clark was born in Mountainburg, Arkansas, on February 26, 1902, and was thirty when he entered Lansing. He had his first brush with the law in 1923 and was sent to the state reformatory at Granite, Oklahoma. First offenders, despite their age, were usually sent to Granite instead of the hard-core main prison at McAlester. Clark was quickly discharged and moved to Texas where he became a farm hand and oil field "boomer," or handyman. But his five-foot eight-and-a-half-inch frame and 140 pounds didn't suit the hard work and he turned to running booze across the border from Mexico. He tried a robbery in Midland, Texas, in 1927, was caught and tossed in jail for thirty days. In 1928, he moved back to Oklahoma and on March 31 received a five-year sentence on another unsuccessful robbery. He served less than a year and was released only to wind up on March 14, 1932, sentenced to three years for stealing a cow in his native Sequoyah County, Oklahoma. On May 25, 1932, he simply walked away from the Colby prison camp, where he was serving as a trusty.

Davis had always been out of touch with society. As a youth he was perpetually in trouble with the law. Born in Waurika, Oklahoma, on July 30, 1900, he joined the army at seventeen but was released a short time later on January 2, 1918. Unemployed and unskilled, he became a wanderer, finally returned to the Waurika area in the summer of 1919. He and two companions, Oscar Steelman and Earl Berry, held up Earl Vanbibber and then broke into the home of S. L. Hollister at nearby Addington, Oklahoma. They were nabbed and Davis was given a two-year sentence to the state reformatory at Granite. By midsummer 1920, he was discharged.

He hit the rails, catching a freight train into Kansas. At Hutchinson, a railroad detective turned him over to local authorities where he was charged with "train riding" and carrying a concealed weapon. The charges were dismissed when he agreed to get out of town, which he did by grabbing another freight.

On January 23, 1923, he teamed with Bill Sheppard to rob a Rush Springs, Oklahoma, oilman named Joe McDonald of $50, a $125 watch, and diamond rings valued at $2,300. McDonald was nailed in his garage as he was leaving for work. The holdup men ordered him to remain in his car for fifteen minutes after they fled down an alley. However, a heavy snowfall the night before held prints for lawmen to follow. The robbers were tracked to a house in Agawam, a community five miles to the north. Davis and Sheppard admitted their guilt before Judge Cham Jones, who gave them ten years in McAlester.

Davis was released in five years. By the spring of 1930, he was back in trouble with the law. He was nabbed in Clark County, Arkansas, and the state police threw him in jail in Little Rock. He served a short term and headed for Texas, where he was in and out of county jails in Howard, Midland, Eastland, and Crosby counties for robberies in the towns of Crane, Midland, Sterling City, and Dawson. Then he went to Nebraska and capped off the year with jail time in Columbus for a robbery attempt there.

Davis was normally a quiet man and somewhat of a loner. An ear ailment was affecting his hearing and he became highly irritable. His fellow robbers were aware that when Davis held a gun a severe personality change occurred. When armed, he became wild-eyed, and even his companions feared he'd shoot them if the occasion arose. Yet in all his crimes, he'd never shot anyone—until 1931.

On April 20, 1931, J. R. Hill, police officer of Marlow, Oklahoma, and Ike Veach, night police chief, checked a 1930 Ford with three men inside about 2 a.m. The car had been driven slowly around town, then parked south of Main Street on Seminole Avenue, when the officers approached. As soon as the patrol car stopped, two shotgun blasts tore into its windshield. Hill was killed instantly and Veach received pellets in the forefinger, left leg, and scalp. He lunged against Hill, the door swung open, and the two tumbled to the pavement. One more blast failed to hit them as the Ford roared away into the night. Veach managed to fire one shot at the car, hitting one of the gunmen. Two and a half blocks away, the accidental discharge of a gun tore through the floorboards and disabled the intake manifold, which caused the car to quit running. The killers placed their injured companion on the curbing, halted another Ford, driven by W. B. Lee, Jr., of Purcell, Oklahoma, who, along with a passenger, helped the wounded man into their car. They then sped south on Highway 81. A few miles from town, the gunmen attempted to halt a northbound Buick, but at first the driver wouldn't stop. A volley of gunshots changed his mind and the two gunmen transferred their wounded companion into the larger car. Later, in the abandoned Ford, officers found a .38 Spanish pistol, a hand drill used to punch safes, fuse cord and other safe-cracking equipment, plus skillets and camping utensils.

Davis quickly determined Oklahoma was too hot. He picked up his wife and drove to Texas. Midway between Joinerville and Turnersville, they found a house to rent. On the night of April 24, just four days after the killing in Marlow, Texas rangers grabbed a suspect, "Paul Martin," twenty-eight, in an oil-field rooming house near Henderson, Texas. Jack Allred, who was the wounded member of the trio, was also captured and placed in the Duncan, Oklahoma, hospital to await trial. The next day, Sheriff E.R. Young raided the Davis house and took him into custody. He and Martin were returned to Oklahoma and placed in the Duncan jail for safekeeping. It turned out Paul Martin was really John Schrimsher, one of Davis's old Waurika buddies. Davis, Allred, and Schrimsher began life sentences in McAlester on August 3, 1931.

The following May 26, Davis, Robert Smith, and Edmond Hardin were among a crew of twenty convicts working on a plastering job in the women's ward at McAlester, about a mile west of the main prison building. They discovered a saw among the tools, sawed through the bars on a second floor, and dropped to the ground. A torrential rainstorm had muffled the sound of the sawing. The escapees slogged to a chain-link fence, found an unlocked gate, and followed a small ditch across the prison farm to a point near a coal mine. The rain obscured their flight until they grabbed a car near the mine. Guards Sherman Shephard and Bill Mullen captured Hardin, but Davis and Smith got away. Near the town of Haywood, they ran their stolen auto across railroad tracks to get onto Highway 270. Pursuers lost them there.

Sawyer also was an Oklahoma farm boy. Born near Durant, Oklahoma, on May 1, 1899, he was named James Franklin Sawyer by his father, Frank, and mother, Rebecca, who reared three boys and six girls with a highly respectable Baptist upbringing. Young Frank was the fourth child in the part-Indian family.

When he was seventeen, Frank met Jim Baldwin and Tom Slaughter at a country dance. They were a couple of wild ones and convinced Sawyer he should join them in robbing some small-town banks in the vicinity. It was great excitement in an otherwise routine farm life. But one night the elder Sawyer noted his favorite saddle horse had been ridden hard, and when he uncovered a money sack in the manger, he confronted young Frank. The youth confessed his involvement and volunteered to return the money. His father wanted to inform the sheriff, but his mother felt the shame would be too hard on the rest of the family. Frank was told to leave home. He headed for the oil fields around Tulsa, where work was plentiful for strong, willing farm boys. By the time he was eighteen, he'd become a card dealer in the oil-boom gambling joints. He moved to Wichita, Kansas, to a swankier club late in 1917. While working there he met Jeff Davis, Henry Wells, and Bud Maxwell, three well-known bank robbers. He joined forces with them for about a year, hitting some small banks around Coffeyville, Kansas, and Oklahoma's Osage Hills. When he turned nineteen in 1918, Sawyer received notice of impending induction into the armed forces. He returned home to Durant for a few days before reporting to Denison, Texas, just across the border from his home county. While being processed, the Armistice was signed and he was released. He returned to Wichita, went to Coffeyville for a time, and then to Nowata, Oklahoma, where he returned to gambling as a profession.

A job in Claremore, Oklahoma, opened up and Sawyer moved again. There he met Al Spencer, who ranked with Belle Starr as one of the more notorious bank robbers in the state's history. While a member of Spencer's gang, he was accused of cheating in a card game by a bank robber named John Moore. Moore wound up dead in the gunfight that followed. Pleading self-defense, Sawyer was acquitted but the trouble forced him to leave the area. He went back to Durant. He found a card game, but Sawyer thought the dealer, a professional named Bleaker, was cheating. In the argument that followed, Bleaker was killed. Sawyer fled town, was nailed in Dallas six months later and returned to Oklahoma for trial. He was sentenced to life from his native Bryan County.

Sawyer was received at McAlester to start his sentence

on April 13, 1920. He escaped in mid-1922, headed directly for Wynona, the home of his old friend, Al Spencer. Wynona in 1922 was a booming oil town. In the midst of the Osage Indian reservation, the hamlet swelled overnight to a brawling, free-wheeling, spirited town of drillers, gamblers, prostitutes, and drifters.

Shortly after Sawyer rejoined his old boss, Spencer made a deal to dispose of some Liberty bonds through a fence. When Spencer, Sawyer, and the fence met, it developed the fence was actually a federal marshal. Spencer drew a gun, as did the marshal. The veteran outlaw fell mortally wounded in an exchange of shots. Sawyer escaped.

A sidelight to Spencer's death was of considerable interest to his friends. An informant who set Spencer up for the marshal received a reward and hurried home to display the wad to his wife. As he opened the door, his wife blasted him with a shotgun. She had just discovered he'd been running around with another woman.

In 1923, Sawyer got married. His bride tried desperately but unsuccessfully to get him to quit his gambling ways. Even the birth of a daughter failed to convert him to the straight and narrow life. Shortly after his daughter arrived, Sawyer was caught in Oklahoma City and returned to McAlester to continue his life term.

On February 2, 1930, the prison sent a number of convicts to Oklahoma City to paint the capitol building. To house the men, a large tent was staked out. Sawyer slipped out of the tent and was free again. He hung around Oklahoma City for the next two years, gambling and sticking up stores to make his living. On May 2, 1932, he and a companion robbed the little bank and post office in Union of $1,300. He then met Clark and Davis, and the ill-fated trip to Missouri followed.

By the time Bailey arrived at Lansing in August, the other three involved in the Fort Scott case had settled into the prison routine. The Kansas penitentiary was considered the best in the Midwest by veteran lawbreakers because of the good food. Most of the products consumed by the inmates were grown on the prison farm, and convicts sought to be assigned to the farm details, which were, of course, outside the walls. Since the prison population of eighteen hundred inmates included five hundred farmers, nearly four hundred laborers, and more than a hundred mechanics, it was obvious the farm had adequate staffing available. Each morning, the work details for the farm assembled and marched in groups through the gates for daytime work in the fields in the fertile valley of the Kansas River (known locally as the Kaw), where the prison was located.

Incidentally, further statistics about the prisoners indicated about fifteen hundred were white, over two hundred black. Seventy percent said the reason they were behind bars was because they needed money, and about ten percent said liquor was the reason. Just under a hundred had been convicted of bank robbery and about the same number for murder. Less than half acknowledged a church affiliation. Most of the prisoners were Kansans, but a surprising number were from Oklahoma, nearly three hundred. Medically, thirty percent of all inmates had positive Wasserman tests, but only two percent were addicted to drugs. Oddly, nearly one hundred had college educations.

None of the Fort Scott foursome received the desired farm jobs. Clark was assigned to the mines, Bailey and Davis worked in the twine plant, and Sawyer was a clean-up man in the prison barbershop.

The arrival of Bailey, with his outside contacts, galvanized Clark into action with his escape plans.

## The Overalls Shipment

Big Bob Brady slid back the heavy boxcar door. The cold
Kansas prairie wind whipped at his clothing as he peered
into the darkness. He made out the flickering coal-oil lamps
in the shacks alongside the Rock Island Railroad tracks.
Turning to a companion huddled in a corner of the rattling
boxcar, Brady bent over to pick up a suitcase held together
with a piece of cord.

"Come on, Frank, this is Liberal. Let's get off here,"
Brady announced.

The train slowed to a crawl, and Brady swung his six-
foot one-inch frame over the side, dropped the last few feet
to the cinders below. His companion followed and the pair
made their way to a dirt road alongside the railroad right-
of-way.

As they approached the railroad station, Brady noticed a
faded sign, illuminated by a single bulb, hanging in front
of a building behind the station. He could barely discern

the word "Rooms" on the gently swinging sign, keeping time to the chilling wind sweeping in from the Colorado Rockies. As the pair neared the building, Brady could make out two other signs, one indicating they were on Kansas Street and the other indicating the rooms for rent were above George's Grocery. They climbed the rickety staircase and were greeted by a sleepy-eyed clerk, who proffered the register.

"Rooms is fifty cents, in advance," the old man advised. Brady fished a dollar bill from his mackinaw jacket.

The next morning, Brady looked around for a car to steal.

"Let's get a new one from some dealer," Brady suggested to his companion. "We can always pick up some plates for it."

The pair first went to the Liberal Auto Supply, a Ford dealership, but the manager, C. C. Bradford, was busy with another customer. As the roughly dressed duo waited, they chatted with an office secretary, Etta Larue. A Seward County sheriff's car cruised by. The officer waved at Bradford.

"We'll be back later, miss," Brady told the secretary. The pair casually sauntered to the street, watching the patrol car as it continued its route.

At the Hood Motor Company, they asked to see a new Plymouth. The owner, L. O. Hood, personally waited on the prospective customers. It was October 1, 1932, a day L. O. Hood would long remember.

"Howdy," the big man greeted the smiling Hood. "We're a couple of farmers from up northwest of here and we're looking for a new car. We'd like a demonstration ride if you don't mind."

"Yes sir, gentlemen," the car dealer answered. "I think you'll find these Plymouths have the finest braking system of any car on the market. Let's try this blue sedan over here."

Hood drove north of town a few miles. Suddenly, Brady produced a pistol and ordered Hood to pull off on a side road.

"Frank, I'm gonna take the car back into town and fill up. You keep our pal here covered until I get back," Brady announced. "Frank" was never identified, but was thought to be Frank Philpott, twenty-six, from Noble, Oklahoma. He remained on the country road with Hood until Brady returned. Hood was ordered into the back seat, and Brady drove west, then south, bypassing Liberal before picking up Highway 54 at Tyrone, Oklahoma.

Brady pulled a cigar from his inside coat pocket, then turned to offer one to his unwilling passenger.

"Want an El Producto?"

Hood declined.

Brady continued to drive the Plymouth southwest along Highway 54 until he reached the town of Hooker. Wanting to avoid Guymon, he turned off 54 onto a country road, and at the Texas border, near the hamlet of Hitchland, he halted the car by a maize field.

"You can get out here, mister," Brady told his captive. "But let's have your shoes first." When Hood slipped off his shoes, Brady flung them into the maize field.

"That ought to slow you down a little," Brady laughed, then drove on into Texas. The Panhandle of Oklahoma is less than fifty miles wide between Liberal and the Texas border, so Hood was not far from home. He called his family from Hitchland to let them know he was safe.

Brady and Frank arrived in Las Vegas, New Mexico, about eight hours later. After spending two days there, they ran out of money. They decided to return to their native Oklahoma, but needed cash for food and fuel. They stopped at Springer, New Mexico, gave the bank a cursory casing, and held it up on October 4. They abandoned the Plymouth, stole another, and headed back home to the Sooner State.

In the meantime, two irate sheriffs were pooling efforts to find Brady. O. L. Clark of Guymon and Brady were enemies since the day the former Blanchard, Oklahoma, farm boy jumped a deputy in the Texas County jail. Brady and Clarence "Buck" Adams had held up the First National Bank of Texhoma (which was in Clark's county) and taken $5,300 on September 15, 1931. Clark tracked the bandits to New Mexico. He nabbed them on September 26 coming out of the Carlsbad Caverns, while dozens of tourists looked on. Clark rushed his prisoners to Amarillo, where he placed them in the city jail for safekeeping overnight.

The jail was situated so that prisoners could visit with passers-by on the street. Brady, the garrulous type, whiled away the time talking to a number of citizens during his short stay. Clark returned the pair to the Guymon jail the following day. Then, several days later, Brady grabbed a deputy who was serving breakfast, wrestled his gun from him, and slammed him against the cellblock. Adams held the deputy through the bars. While Brady was rummaging through a desk drawer to find the key to release Adams, the deputy broke loose and pulled a small-caliber pistol from his boot top. Brady turned in time to catch a bullet just below his left eye. It passed through the skull and exited below the ear, missing the brain by a fraction. He was rushed to the nearest hospital, the Epworth Hospital in Liberal, where he quickly recovered. The only permanent damage was an inability to lower the left eyelid, and he was forced to wear glasses thereafter. Even in sleep the left eye never closed, and it was often said in jest that the law couldn't catch Brady because he slept with one eye open.

A month later, following his conviction for the Texhoma robbery, Brady was back in the state penitentiary at McAlester, where he had served time in 1922 for forgery and again in 1925 for armed robbery in Nowata County. On July 23, 1932, he instituted one of the most inspired escapes in the state's history.

Brady was working in the prison overalls shop, which provided work clothes for the depression-wracked farmers at a reduced cost. The overalls were packed for shipping in huge wooden crates. Each morning, a truck hauled the crates outside the walls. Brady fashioned a cardboard box inside one of the crates, crawled into it one Saturday morning, pulled the crate lid shut with a rope attached to the cover, and waited to be loaded on the truck. The convicts loading the crates noticed the additional weight of Brady's 187 pounds inside, so they purposely put the crate next to the truck's gate. Once outside the prison, Brady released the lid, jumped out of the moving truck. The driver never knew a thing. Brady chose Saturday for his escape so his absence wouldn't be noted until Monday morning when he failed to show up for work. By that time, it was too late for the prison bloodhounds to be used.

Following his escape, Brady picked up his twenty-one-year-old wife, Leona, in Oklahoma city, and they went to visit her parents in Des Moines, Iowa. He used the name "Leonard R. Gray" and posed as a salesman. Leona's seventeen-year-old sister, Frances Defer, never suspected her smooth-talking, good-humored brother-in-law was a bank robber, forger and burglar.

In August, 1932, the Bradys returned to Oklahoma. Brady, for the second time in his career, robbed the bank at Ada, where a brother operated a real-estate firm. He then went to Missouri to hit the El Dorado Springs bank.

While her husband was doing his jobs in Oklahoma and Missouri, Leona moved to Des Moines, first to 1205 Woodland and then to 1301 Highland. Her parents lived at 824 Pleasant.

After the Hood affair, Sheriffs O. L. Clark and Gene Worden began their search for Brady at Hollis, Oklahoma, where Leona had lived at the time of the Texhoma robbery. It was discovered she had moved to Oklahoma City, but neighbors believed she had again moved to Des Moines.

The sheriffs notified the Des Moines police department, who began watching the houses where the Defer family resided. On December 19, in front of the residence at 1301 Highland, police noticed a car with Texas plates parked alongside the curb. As they watched, two women and a man answering Brady's description left the house and entered the car. Des Moines detectives Loren Miller, Fred Sillick, and Charles Antrim halted the trio. Brady casually unbuttoned his top-coat, but was ordered to throw up his hands. A .38-caliber pistol was tucked in his waistband, and a search of the car revealed a rifle and ammunition under the seat. In his pocket, "Leonard Gray" had a deputy sheriff's badge that bore the name Luther Prince, Pontotoc County, Oklahoma.

Sheriff Worden, Undersheriff Logan Graham, and Hood rushed to Des Moines to take custody of the prisoner, as sheriffs from Ada, Oklahoma, and Diamond, Texas, also sought to pick up Brady once word was flashed he had been caught.

On the morning of December 20, the Worden group arrived in Des Moines, signed a release for the prisoner, and immediately left for the return trip to Liberal. They stopped overnight at Manhattan, Kansas, where Brady was placed in the city jail. After a slow, icy trip, they arrived in Liberal. Charges of kidnapping, auto theft, and possession of firearms were entered, and bond was set at $20,000. More than two hundred persons showed up for the arraignment on January 5, where bond was increased to $22,500. When the wire services described Brady as one of the most dangerous men in the Southwest, hundreds of curious farmers from western Kansas drove to Liberal to watch the trial. Oddly, when the jury list was called, L. O. Hood's name was drawn.

A jury deliberated two and a half hours, found the defendant guilty, and Judge F. O. Random sentenced Brady to life as an habitual. He arrived in Lansing two days later.

Brady, whose first record at age fifteen resulted in confinement in the state reformatory at Hutchinson, Kansas, in 1919 on a grand larceny count, had graduated to the Kansas big house. In less than five months he'd be one of the leaders in the most daring escape in Kansas penal history.

# The Tri-State Terror

The instant the door of the Boulevard Club at 512 Southwest Boulevard swung open, bartender Carl Saragusa feared trouble. He recognized the man entering as Wilbur Underhill, the dreaded "Tri-State Terror." Like others outside the law, Underhill frequented the Southwest Boulevard speakeasies when in Kansas City. Most of the bank robbers and thieves who came in to drink or gamble were unobtrusive, but Underhill was different. He generated fear by his very presence.

"Hi, Mr. Underhill, what'll you have?" Saragusa ventured, mopping an imaginary wet spot on the bar.

"Give me a shot and the same for my nephew here," the killer said, pointing toward a nineteen-year-old youth who had entered with him.

As Saragusa poured the shots, Underhill motioned with his right hand to the ceiling. The club's gambling parlor was on the second floor.

"Anybody upstairs?" he asked.

"Some of the boys were up there earlier, but I think they went over to the Horn Inn a while ago," the barkeep replied, realizing his bosses, Joe and Sam Capra, weren't keen about his discussing the customers.

Underhill gulped down his whiskey and turned to his nephew: "Frankie, we better hit the road." He counted out exact change for the two drinks and moved toward the door. The Tri-State Terror wasn't much for tipping.

The glaring summer sun bounced its rays off the sidewalk in front of the club, and the two men wasted no time getting into a blue Ford parked at curbside. They drove away quickly to vent the stifling heat in the car. It was August 11, 1931, and a scorching hot day.

Underhill and his nephew drove to the little Kansas town of Cherryvale, where they checked into a hotel. The previous July 26, Underhill had stayed at the same hotel while waiting for papers to clear for the purchase of a new car. He had told the car salesman he had just been released from the Oklahoma state prison (actually he had escaped), thus had no identification papers. He filed an application for a driver's license and registered the car under the name of "Ralph Carraway." While waiting for the license to return from the state offices in Topeka, Underhill drove to nearby Coffeyville, where he robbed a movie theater of $300. It happened to be "Bank Nite," a popular depression-era promotion for motion-picture houses.

Early on the morning of August 12, the pair left Cherryvale and drove to Wichita. Underhill looked around for a filling station to rob, finally choosing a Texaco station at Kellogg and Ida. At 9:45 p.m., he and Frank pulled into the driveway.

Before the youthful attendant could say a word, Underhill pointed a .45 revolver in his direction.

"I ain't got much, mister, it's been a slow night." The youth proved it, emptying his coverall pockets. He handed over $14.68.

Underhill was furious.

"I oughtta kill you, kid," he yelled, his cold gray eyes riveted on the youth's face.

"Honest, mister, that's all I got."

Just then a car drove up for service. Underhill gnashed the Ford's gears and roared away. A few blocks away, speeding through an intersection, Underhill's car collided with one driven by J. A. Walker of Fairview, Oklahoma. The Ford was damaged severely and had to be towed to the Lucas Garage at 125 South Water Street. The Underhills walked to the Iris Hotel, at Water and Douglas, and checked in shortly before 2 a.m.

Police officer Merle Colver, forty-seven, was assigned the downtown hotel beat. His job was to check newly arrived strangers in the dingy hotels of Wichita. The name "Ralph Carraway" on the Iris register was a strange one to Colver. He obtained a passkey from the desk and walked to Room 204. He rapped sharply twice, then let himself into the room.

"Hi, boys," the smiling officer said, "It's my job to check out residents of the hotel. Got any identification?"

The sleepy-eyed Underhill arose and began struggling with his trousers. Colver sat on the foot of the bed. Underhill pulled out a wallet, handed the officer his driver's license. Several photographs dropped from the wallet on the bed in the process. Underhill then slipped on his shirt and walked behind Colver as if to pick up his shoes. Suddenly he whipped out a .45-caliber pistol from his pants pocket and placed it next to Colver's head. Three shots rang out. Colver's blood splattered over Underhill's chest and arms. As the officer fell forward, Underhill fired twice more, both bullets tearing chunks of wood from the floor. Young Frank stood in open-mouthed shock as Underhill tore off his bloody shirt, grabbed his coat, and ran to the door.

"Come on, Frankie," he screamed. The youngster followed as Underhill raced down the hallway and into the alley behind the hotel.

They ran until they reached a park, where they spent the rest of the day in hiding. The entire 150-man police force was assigned to the search for the cop killers. At dusk, Underhill and his nephew emerged from the park. Two officers spotted the pair and ordered them to halt. Underhill had his coat slung over his arm and was bare chested, not unusual for people in a park. Two .45 revolvers were pocketed in the coat. When he heard the order to halt, he began to run, all the while groping for the guns.

Officer Jack Myler fired a warning shot at the fleeing pair, with tragic consequences. The bullet passed over their heads and struck a two-year-old boy sitting on a porch. Little Don George Colliate, hit in the arm and side, was killed instantly.

Myler's second shot hit Underhill in the neck, paralyzing his right arm. The coat, heavy with the guns, dropped to the ground. Underhill kept running despite his serious injury. Four blocks later, he collapsed. Frank, who was unarmed, offered no resistance.

Underhill was taken to jail and bond was set at $2,000. He quickly recovered from his wound. At his trial, the photographs that had fallen from his wallet in the hotel room were presented. One showed Underhill and his wife, Lucille, taken at Heavener, Oklahoma. Heavener lawmen verified Underhill had lived for a time in the town and did have a wife named Lucille. There was little doubt the man captured in the park and the murderer of Colver were the same person. Underhill was sentenced to life imprisonment at Lansing, where he arrived on September 4, 1931.

(No charges were placed against Frank Underhill, who never again got in trouble with the law.)

Underhill was unquestionably a dangerous psychopath. His mother, Nancy Almira Underhill, explained that as a youngster he had been injured, and: "I don't think it left him quite right." Growing up on the streets of Joplin, Missouri, young Wilber (he changed the spelling to Wilbur in later years because he thought it was more masculine) was a regular churchgoer. His father, also named Wilber, had a police record and his three brothers, Earl, George, and Ernest—all older—were criminals. Each served time at the Missouri state prison. His four sisters were hard-working, law-abiding girls. The three youngest married well. Dorothy, the oldest, took care of their mother until she died.

Wilbur's first brush with the Joplin police came when he was accused of stealing silverware from a house. He told police he had just finished helping a church janitor sweep out and was walking home when a stranger stopped him.

"The man said he'd walk with me and when we got in front of this house, he said to wait a minute and he'd be back," the youngster told police. "He came back with a bunch of stuff. The cops came a few minutes later."

The police let young Underhill go with some advice about not trusting strangers.

In 1919, when he was eighteen, Underhill received his first official record. He was charged with burglary. He soon joined his brothers at the Missouri state prison. Ernest was doing life for killing a hot-tamale vendor in Joplin in 1913. George and Earl were convicted burglars. The boys' father was dead by this time, leaving their mother and the four girls to fend for themselves. Dorothy, who had taken a business course in high school, told her mother she was committed to caring for her the rest of her life. To escape the stigma attached to the Underhill name, they moved to Kansas City, where Dorothy obtained employment as a secretary. The other girls remained in Joplin, forced to drop out of school and work to support themselves.

When Wilbur was released from prison, he had just turned twenty-one. He resumed his occupation as burglar. By 1923, he had become the "Lover's Lane Bandit," preying on parked couples in the various necking areas around Joplin. He was apprehended when police set up decoys. Again, he was sent to Jefferson City to join his brothers.

After serving nearly four years of a five-year sentence, he was released in the fall of 1926.

On Christmas night, 1926, he and Ike "Skeet" Akins entered the Purity Drug Store in Okmulgee, Oklahoma, displayed guns, and ordered nineteen-year-old George Fee to stick up his hands. The young man either froze in fear or simply was slow to react. Underhill, without additional warning, began firing, killing Fee instantly. The bandits fled without taking any money.

Sheriff John Russell of Okmulgee County began trailing the pair. First, he tracked them to Tulsa, where informants told him Underhill and Akins had left for Kansas City, Kansas. The trail then shifted to Webb City, Missouri, back to Okmulgee, and then to Wichita. Finally, on January 7, 1927, in Tulsa, they were captured. In Underhill's possession was a pistol identified as one stolen from W. H. Hastings, a conductor for the Southwest Missouri Railroad, an interurban line, in Baxter Springs, Kansas. Underhill was returned to Okmulgee County custody for the Fee murder.

Underhill's friends smuggled him hacksaw blades and he sawed his way out of the jail several weeks later. He surfaced in the mining town of Picher, Oklahoma, where he shot a sixteen-year-old boy, Fred Smythe, in a street robbery. Later, again in Picher, he was spotted, and in a shoot-out on the street, he accidentally killed a bystander, Earl O'Neal, a miner. He fled to Tulsa and again was captured and returned to the Okmulgee jail. Quickly tried this time, he was sentenced to life. He arrived at McAlester on June 7, 1927.

His mental condition deteriorated behind bars. Within weeks after being incarcerated, he tried an escape and was thrown into solitary confinement. His perpetual escape schemes were ignored by fellow inmates, who recognized his insanity. Finally, after four years behind bars, on July 14, 1931, he escaped. While working on a road gang, something diverted the attention of one of the gun-toting guards and Underhill slipped into the underbrush. His absence was quickly discovered and a search flushed him. He ran toward a nearby river, miraculously escaping the fusillade of shots. He reached the river, jumped in, and, as bullets plunked the water around him, swam to the opposite bank and safety.

He was nearly captured months later in the little Oklahoma town of Panama. He received a gunshot wound in the left arm but slipped away.

He lived by robbing filling stations, grocery stores, and an occasional motion-picture theater. On occasion, he visited a young lady in Independence, Kansas, named Ethyl, whom he later claimed to have married, but no record has been found to substantiate the marriage. Finally, he collected enough loot to buy a car. A friend drove him to Cherryvale, Kansas, for that purpose.

Inside the walls of Lansing following the killing of Policeman Colver in Wichita, Underhill's insanity became more apparent. He bickered with other inmates, showed an obsessive hatred for all law officers, and ruled the prison population with a handful of toughs who followed him about. He extorted cigarettes from other prisoners, as well as booze they made in the mines. Most of the guards feared him. He openly stated several times that someday he'd kill the warden, Kirk Prather. When George Underhill, Wilbur's closest brother, took an overdose of sodium amobarbital, a barbiturate, and died on November 7, 1931, Wilbur asked permission to attend the funeral in Joplin. Prather, of course, denied it. Underhill went into a rage and was sent to solitary confinement for a fourth time in the sixty days he'd been in Lansing. Prather became so fearful of Underhill, he installed a gas bomb above his office door as extra protection.

The arrival of Bailey several months later further upset Underhill. He felt the biggest name among the prison inmates represented a threat to his convict leadership. He watched closely as the "king of bandits" developed an entourage of his own. Bailey was actually looked at in awe by a number of the prison officials and many of the inmates, and Underhill was furious. He reacted with another strong-arm attempt on the population.

Granted permission to visit the warden, Underhill tromped into Prather's office.

"Warden, my mother is sick and needs help. I want to pass the hat among the boys and get some cash to pay her doctor's bills," he demanded.

Prather surely was aware the request was nothing more than a guise to shake down the prisoners, yet he gave permission. There is no record of how much Underhill and his thugs forced out of the other prisoners, but it was most likely a goodly amount.

Underhill's next ploy was to plan a break. As usual with his schemes, this one was known to every guard and inmate within hours. His plan involved smuggling guns inside the walls in bales of sisal hemp shipped in for the twine plant. Ironically, his plot was camouflaging another break being planned by Jim Clark and Bob Brady.

## The Plot

Jim Clark leaned against the brick wall of the prison hospital. He reached for the string of a Bull Durham tobacco sack that hung from his striped-denim shirt pocket. Slowly, he poured the finely shredded tobacco into a cigarette paper held in his left hand. His watery blue eyes stared at the heavy steel gates that sealed the administration building from the prison interior. With a sudden flick of his wrist, the tag on the end of the string flipped in the air and Clark caught it with his teeth. Tugging on the sack with his hand as his clenched teeth held the string fast, he eased the tobacco sack shut, all the while rolling the cigarette with his left hand.

He scanned the gates carefully, then let his gaze drift down the brick pathway that led from the administration building, past the officers' dining hall, the boiler plant, and the hospital, before emptying into the recreation yard. The strip of brick paving was called "Broadway" by inmates and guards alike, a title given to the main thoroughfare in many prisons.

Clark's searching eyes paused momentarily on the twine plant, located north of the baseball diamond. Slowly, the wiry Oklahoman turned his attention to the yellow, gray, and brown limestone wall that surrounded the prison. He concentrated on the guard tower, Number 3½, which hovered above the third-base foul line. He could easily make out the guard, a stove, a coat rack, and a broom in the turret. About a hundred yards to the south was Tower Number 3, situated in the extreme southeast corner of the prison. Access to Number 3 was gained through an iron door directly below, facing center field of the baseball diamond. Clark's gaze stopped on the iron gate, the only opening in the big wall other than the main gate.

"That's the way outta this damn place," he said to himself.

He measured the limestone walls with his eyes.

"Must be twenty-five feet high," he thought. "No way over that baby. Gotta go through that door."

Clark took a long drag on his cigarette, flipped it into the cinders alongside the brick paving, and moved toward his cell.

For the next few days, all of Clark's thinking time was centered on the iron door. He utilized much of his free time during the day striving to develop an escape plan. His work detail was in the prison coal mine, where he tended the mules used to haul the heavy carts the inmate miners filled with coal. Clark fed the animals and watered them each morning and again at the conclusion of the workday. In between, he had little to do except on those occasions when one of the mules, blinded by years of darkness, was injured.

Spring had come to Kansas, and outside the walls, warm rains were making quagmires of the dirt farm-to-market roads. As April turned into May, motorists found themselves restricted mainly to the paved roads, State Highway 5 and U.S. 73E in particular. Highway 5 skirted the prison farm area to the east while the heavier-traveled 73E passed directly in front of the prison gates, about three hundred yards west.

On the extreme eastern edge of the prison farm, a spur line of the Union Pacific Railroad skirted the property. Where Highway 5 crossed the tracks, a small yellow depot stood. Although only one train chugged through the hills to Leavenworth each day, and none on Sundays or holidays, the Union Pacific kept a station agent on duty every day. The solo train returned to Kansas City's yards at dusk, stopping at the Lansing station for freight and an occasional passenger.

Highway 5 wound its way beside the Missouri River to Wolcott, thence on to Kansas City, Kansas. With the "Big Muddy" to the north, all roads branching from the highway took a southerly route, eventually ending on the east-west routes, Kansas 32 or the larger, paved U.S. 40.

From Topeka, the state capital, came word that the new Republican governor, Alfred M. Landon, had begun his housecleaning. Warden Kirk Prather, an appointee of the departed governor, Harry Woodring, was to be replaced on June 1 by Lacey Simpson, a farmer from Canton, Kansas, who had been active in Landon's campaign. When word of Prather's firing reached the inmates, Clark instantly realized this was his opportunity to escape. He went to work seriously on his plan.

Meanwhile, Underhill was also lining up cohorts for another break-out try. He had tried twice before, failing both times to get his plans past the talking stage. Two years before, he convinced fellow convicts Jim Morris, Glen Belfield, Lee Myers, Orville Haines, J. B. Knight, Francis Sharp, and Alva "Sonny" Payton they could overpower the guards and blast their way out. The plot was uncovered and the plotters were tossed into solitary confinement. Undeterred, Underhill tried again. He used urine as invisible ink and wrote a friend, asking him to smuggle in some guns. A prison censor noted the wide spaces between the lines of writing and held the paper to the light. He spotted the secret message in the spaces and Underhill got more time in the hole.

Underhill's latest plot involved kidnapping the warden and forcing his way out the front gate with Prather as a shield. Prather got wind of the plot, but since he was leaving in a few days, ignored the report.

The inmates soon became aware of Prather's declining interest in his job. He spent considerable time away from the prison, often driving to nearby Kansas City, Kansas, his home town, to seek a new job. The depression made even political jobs scarce, and Democrats were hard pressed to find work under the new Republican administration in Kansas. Clark thought Prather's lackadaisical attitude would benefit an escape attempt. He cornered his old friend from the Oklahoma state prison days, Big Bob Brady.

"Bob, we gotta get outta this damn joint," he whispered. "I got a plan."

Brady's face lit up. A veteran of three other escapes, he delighted in the prospect of going over the wall.

"Here's the deal," Clark went on. "The day Prather gets his ass out of here, he's a cinch to make the rounds and tell everybody good-bye. When he does, we grab him as a hostage, take him through that gate in center field and over the wall. We need some guns and at least a couple more guys. And we gotta work fast, 'cause that new warden comes in June first. Prather will really be taking it easy until then."

Brady listened intently, nodded his agreement.

"Them guns are gonna be hard to get," Brady stated. "They'll cost money and I ain't got two goddam dimes to rub together."

"Christ, we can get the money. Old Man Bailey's got a shit-pot full of it," Clark surmised.

"Well, that crazy son of a bitch Underhill can probably get the guns if we can get the cash. I'll try him out." Brady, one of the few inmates who didn't fear Underhill, quickly approached the killer about obtaining the necessary guns.

"Hell, man, I can get anything in here if you got the money," Underhill laughed. "I got contacts in Wichita that can get any damn thing you want."

"We can get the cabbage, don't worry none about that," Brady responded, not sure just how Clark planned to raise the funds, but confident in his friend's ability.

Assured of the source for the guns, Clark and Brady went about finding the money. They approached Harvey Bailey in the twine plant.

"Harve, you gotta minute?" Clark asked.

"Yeah, boys. What's up?"

"We got a plan to get outta this joint. We thought you might want in," Clark said.

"Sorry, boys. I got a fix on and I'll be out of here in less than a year."

"We was sorta counting on you to provide the dough."

"Well, that might be arranged. What kind of money are you talking about?" Bailey wanted to know.

"Underhill says he can get us four .380s for two hundred bucks," Brady revealed.

"Christ-a-mighty, I don't want nothing to do with that crazy bastard. Deal me out all the way," Bailey countered, turning back to his job.

Clark and Brady tried for several days to interest someone else in putting up the money. Bailey, it seemed, was the only one of the eighteen hundred inmates who had money on the outside. They returned to Bailey with another plea.

"Look, Harve, you are the only one that nut will listen to," Clark pleaded. "If you go along, you can control him.

If you don't, he'll kill that warden before we get out the gate. The warden's our only ticket out of here. If he gets it, we're all dead men."

Bailey knew they were right about Underhill, but still refused to join the plotters.

On May 10, Bailey walked up to Clark in the yard.

"I'll get the dough here in a couple days, but I still ain't going with you," he whispered.

Clark began searching for Brady and located him sitting in the sun outside the mess hall.

"Bob, the Old Man will have the money here in a couple of days. Tell Underhill to send for the guns," Clark whispered.

When Underhill came through the chow line, Brady was waiting for him.

"We got the dough, get the guns," Brady informed him.

Bailey's contact with the outside world was a kitchen helper who unloaded the daily supply truck from Kansas City. The helper informed the driver, who in turn contacted Bailey's niece in Kansas City. Two days later the money was delivered by the truck driver. Underhill smuggled the two hundred dollars to a friend in Wichita, who stashed three revolvers in bales of sisal hemp used in the twine plant. Prison inspection of the bales was sporadic, and the guns were not discovered. Underhill turned them over to Clark and Brady, who had them hidden in the hospital, which seldom was included in the shakedowns.

Clark was convinced two more men were needed for the break.

"Remember those boys that came in with me, Ed Davis and Frank Sawyer?" he asked Brady. "I think they oughtta get to go along. They got no more business in here than I have."

Brady agreed, and when asked, Davis and Sawyer eagerly agreed to join the plot.

"But we still gotta get the Old Man to go along or that crazy Underhill will blow it for all of us," Clark insisted.

Clark repeated his plea to Bailey once more.

"Harvey, he'll do what you tell him. If you don't come along, he'll kill that warden, and the rest of us are goners the minute the warden dies."

Bailey, behind bars for the first time in his life, was beginning to feel the urge for freedom. He agreed to join the break.

Clark's scheme centered on the appearance of Prather at the season opener for the prison baseball team on Memorial Day. Traditionally, the KSP Red Sox played the University of Kansas on May 30. Clark was positive Prather would show up at some point in the game, but if he didn't, the break was to be attempted on June 1, when Prather was to turn over the keys to the new warden. When it was announced the Kansas team had so little practice due to the heavy spring rains that it couldn't appear, two American Legion junior teams from Leavenworth and Topeka were lined up to entertain the prisoners. In order for all inmates to see at least one game, a morning and afternoon double-header was set. Now, Clark was more confident than ever that Prather would have to make an appearance because of the visitors.

Clark passed the word for the plotters to meet in the recreation yard on Sunday afternoon, May 28, to make final plans. Everyone showed up but Sawyer, who didn't get the word. There was always a lot of activity in the barbershop where Sawyer worked and he simply couldn't be reached.

"Boys, we're all set for Tuesday," Clark announced. "Here's what we'll do. I got me a piece of baling wire from the mine to put around the warden's neck so he won't run. Bob has his eye on that ladder in the mess hall they use to wash the walls. As soon as we jump the warden, he'll run get the ladder. I'll wheel that old hayrack parked by the twine plant out while the rest of you take the warden out to Number 3. If the guard won't toss down the keys, we use the ladder and the wagon, which ought to get us high enough to go over the wall."

"Sounds okay by me," Davis said.

"Yeah, I'll blast that warden's ass all over center field if that guard doesn't throw down those keys," Underhill snarled.

"Listen, Wilbur, let's get one thing straight right now," Bailey calmly addressed the killer. "There'll be no gun play at all or else we're all dead men. You keep that damn gun quiet."

Underhill glared at Bailey but said nothing. Bailey's brown eyes never wavered as he returned Underhill's stare. It was apparent the two men were due to clash.

On Monday, May 29, it rained. Bailey recognized this as a severe problem for their getaway, once over the wall.

"Those goddam roads will be a mess," he warned the others. "We'll have to stick to the slab if the cat roads are muddy and that'll be dangerous as hell. They can have a roadblock up in fifteen minutes on those highways."

But by late afternoon of the twenty-ninth, the skies cleared and Bailey's hopes brightened. The roads to the south of the prison would dry quickly since there was a higher clay content in the soil beyond the heavy loam of the Kaw river valley. Once over the wall, the gang would head south to the Cookson Hills of Oklahoma.

The Cooksons offered sanctuary for anyone fleeing from the law. The hilly terrain stretched from near the Kansas border south some seventy-five miles, covered with scrub oak and offering little in the way of agrarian life. The Cherokees who lived in the hills existed by fishing and hunting, with some chicken ranching and a lot of moonshining. The wild, rugged country provided a perfect hideout if one knew the area or had friends there. Underhill had spent time in the Cooksons, mostly in the southern extremes near Vian. Bailey had become acquainted with the hills in the late twenties when he and the part-Choctaw outlaw Pretty Boy Floyd spent some time there. Clark had many friends in the Peggs area, including Marion Pike, who hid him after his prison escape in 1932. Davis, Brady, and Sawyer, as native Oklahomans, had spent enough time in the area to know it well.

Six nervous convicts slept uneasily the night of the twenty-ninth of May. On the morrow, they would attempt the most daring escape in the history of the Kansas State Penitentiary.

# The Break

At 6 a.m. on Memorial Day, 1933, the bell signaling the first breakfast shift at the Kansas state prison sounded. The ponderous steel doors of Cellblock "A" rumbled back, and nine hundred pairs of thick-soled shoes began clomping down the corridors.

Even though it was an official prison holiday, eating routines remained the same. Those in "A" block marched to breakfast promptly at six, along with those assigned to duties other than in the mines or the twine plant, who celled in "C" area. Forty-five minutes later, Cellblock "B" inmates were fed. Feeding eighteen hundred prisoners in the overcrowded facility constituted a major task for prison officials.

Bob Brady, as a member of the kitchen force, had already been at work an hour before the first hungry inmates began lining up at the steam tables. He glanced up from his mopping chores, his brown eyes seeking the familiar forms of

Bailey and Davis, who celled in "A" block. Clark and Underhill were in "B" house and Sawyer bunked in the "C" area with Brady. Brady quickly spotted the six-foot one-inch frame of Bailey in the chow line holding a tin tray waiting for the scrambled eggs, fresh-baked bread, and cornmeal mush to be served. Davis was close behind.

Bailey and Davis made their way toward the center of the huge dining hall, a spot generally reserved for prison big shots. There, as far as possible from the guards posted by the walls, conversation could be conducted with little fear of being overheard. Brady, wiping his damp hands on his apron, sauntered toward his fellow conspirators.

Each table seated eight men, so Brady had to be cautious talking about the planned escape. The rainy days, which made the cat roads all but impassable, had Brady concerned the break might be delayed.

"How's the chow, boys?" Brady opened the conversation.

"Pure horseshit," one of the others at the table responded, forking another load of eggs into his mouth. Bailey continued to eat, not looking toward Brady.

"Looks like the weather cleared," Brady commented, noting the first streaks of sunlight streaming over the high limestone wall that surrounded the prison.

"Yep," Bailey responded. "It's getting real warm, too."

"Wonder if they'll play ball this morning?" Brady wanted to know.

Bailey poised his fork between bites, looked directly at Brady.

"If the sun stays out, things ought to dry up in a hurry," the bank robber declared. Brady caught the meaning.

Satisfied the break was still on, Brady returned to the kitchen. Bailey and Davis finished their meal, walked toward the dining room door where a guard checked to see that each convict returned all three utensils. They stepped out the door onto Broadway.

Following the paved area to the recreation yard, the pair

noted several inmates had already grabbed seats in the stands along the first-base line, waiting for the game to start at nine o'clock. A doubleheader had been scheduled, but the second game, set for 1 p.m., would never be played.

Bailey and Davis picked seats near the backstop just as the bell rang denoting the second breakfast shift was starting. "B" cell inmates marched toward the dining hall. It was 6:45 a.m.

Meanwhile, in his apartment on the second floor of the administration building, Warden Kirk Prather was just awakening. His wife had arisen earlier and the coffeepot was already gurgling on the stove. The warden, a heavy man with a bulbous nose, eased his feet onto the carpet, stretched mightily, and then stood. His mind was filled with concern about his future. In less than two days, his two-year tenure as warden would be over. His replacement, Lacey Simpson, had already toured the facility over the weekend. Although Simpson wouldn't take over officially until June 1, Prather had decided he'd bid early farewells to the guards on duty and the few inmates he cared about and would leave the prison a day ahead to avoid a meeting with Simpson. Prather took little solace in the fact that new Republican governor Alf Landon's landslide win had swept almost every Democrat in the state out of office and that he was not alone among the soon-to-be-unemployed. Sixteen years as a devoted Democratic party worker were going down the drain, the portly warden mused.

He quickly bathed, shaved, and walked to the apartment door to obtain the morning Kansas City *Times.* Breakfast was on the table when he settled to read the paper.

"What time are you leaving for the cemetery?" he asked his wife.

"As soon as I get dressed," she replied. "I want to get there early and then go on into Kansas City. Sure you won't come with me?"

"No, I have some papers to sign and I want to tell the

boys good-bye. Simpson and his wife will be here Thursday to take over and I want to be gone when he gets here."

Prather scanned the *Times* for some mention of his last days as warden. Seeing none, he folded the paper, took a final sip of coffee, patted the family dog, "Skippy," and strode to the door.

"See you this afternoon, dear," he yelled over his shoulder, easing the door shut behind him. He went down the circular iron staircase that led to the floor below, waited for the guard to open the manually operated iron door that separated the office area from the corridor, then walked to his office. A glance noted the gas bomb above the office door was still in place. It was 7:35 a.m. by the clock on his office wall when he walked in.

To the east of the prison was a section reserved for officer housing. A number of trees crowded around the frame buildings. Adjacent to the wall was the prison garage. As a safety measure, any officer living on the grounds who maintained an automobile had to store it in the locked garage overnight. The following morning, a trusty brought the car to each owner's residence, and the trusty, in turn, was driven back to the garage. To the northeast of the grounds lay the prison farm and the dairy barn, both manned by inmates under civilian supervisors. The entire farm program, which produced most of the food for the prison, was supervised by W. W. Woodson, who lived in one of the larger brick homes provided the officers. Although it was a holiday for the remainder of the prison, the farm chores had to be done and Woodson was already on duty when his wife and five children sat down to breakfast. The eldest daughters, Evelyn, twenty-three, and Marion, twenty, usually aided their mother cooking the meals, while the younger children, Virginia, fifteen, Billy, twelve, and Bobby, eight, helped with table-setting and dish-washing duties. Young Bobby could barely wait to get to a stock pond several hundred yards east of the house, where the bluegills were biting.

"Hurry up, Mom," he exclaimed. "It's almost eight o'clock."

Twenty-five miles away in Kansas City, Kansas, in the Union Pacific railroad yards, Milan J. Wood was concluding his shift as a car inspector, a job he'd had for sixteen years. His plans for the holiday included a trip to the cemetery to honor the memory of his grandfather, buried at the National Military Home graveyard at Wadsworth, just north of the state prison grounds. The sun, he noted, was going to produce a warm day. It would be a nice outing for his wife, a semi-invalid, and his seventeen-year-old daughter, Louise. Wood slipped into the dressing room a bit early and when the 8 a.m. whistle blew, denoting the end of his shift, he was already climbing into his brand-new Model 77 Willys sedan. He hoped to get an early start to beat the traffic.

To the southwest of Lansing, in the town of Ottawa, another family was preparing for a holiday outing. Ralph Pettijohn affixed three miniature American flags on the front of his nine-month-old Chevrolet sedan, wiped a bit of dust from the shiny hood, and glanced impatiently toward the house. His eleven-year-old sister, Mabel, was swinging gently in the porch swing, but his wife was still inside, preparing for a trip to the Mount Calvary Cemetery near Lansing. A picnic was planned following the cemetery visit.

Pettijohn slipped in behind the wheel, recorded the odometer reading of 3,656 miles in a book he maintained in the glove compartment, then beeped the horn for his wife.

"Come on, it's eight-thirty already," he shouted, pointing toward a pocket watch he held aloft. Pettijohn worked in a dairy where timing was important to get the daily trucks on the road on schedule.

His wife and young sister climbed into the car and Pettijohn headed for the nearby community of Basehor, where he was to pick up his wife's sister and her husband, Mr. and Mrs. Bert Warren, and their three children.

Promptly at nine o'clock, Coach Bill Meeker sent his Leavenworth Legion team onto the prison field. On the mound was a sixteen-year-old righthander named Murry Dickson, of whom Meeker correctly predicted eventual major-league stardom. The stands were jammed and many of the prisoners stood along the first-base foul line. There were no stands on the third-base side. Wagers of tobacco were being made among the prisoners, and some even had moonshine whiskey, distilled in the mines, to bet. High on the big wall in Tower 3½ down the third-base line, and in Tower 3, in center field, armed officers watched the game begin.

Bailey, Brady, Clark, Davis, and Underhill gathered behind the bleachers. Sawyer, in the barber shop, was one of the few inmates laboring on the holiday. The warden had asked for the barber shop to remain open until he could get a final haircut before departing.

"Okay, boys, things look good," Clark announced. "The warden for damn sure will come by the game sometime this morning. Bob, why don't you go get the guns. I got the wire to put around the warden's neck. Now, remember. Once we get that warden collared, Bob is gonna get the ladder outta the kitchen, I'll get that hay wagon, and just in case we don't get the key to that door, we'll use the wagon and the ladder to go over the wall."

Everyone nodded. Underhill, the excitement already building, was hyperactive. He sparred like a boxer, slapping Davis on the arm several times. Davis slowly turned from the game and stared at the Missourian.

"Listen, you silly son of a bitch. Quit shittin' around or you'll blow this whole thing," he warned Underhill. The two exchanged deadly stares before Davis finally turned his attention back to the baseball game.

Brady returned a short time later with the four .380 automatics tucked in his waistband, hidden by his dungaree shirt. He slipped Bailey, Davis, and Underhill each a gun. Clark was left free to handle the nine-foot-long wire, which he had concealed inside his pants leg. In his waistband, he carried a knife, which he had obtained earlier from its hiding place in the mine where he fed the mules.

As the game progressed, Underhill continued to clown around. Bailey recognized the symptoms. He'd seen kill-crazy men before and he felt Underhill was hyped up with anticipation of killing the warden.

"Underhill, if you shoot that warden, our ticket out of here is gone. I'll blow your head off if you kill him," the bank robber warned.

"Listen, Old Man. Once we get over that wall"—nodding toward center field—"I'm going to shoot his fat ass."

"We'll need him for a hostage until we get to the Cooksons," Bailey reiterated. "Just keep your finger off that trigger."

An hour passed and the warden still didn't show up. Clark was beginning to show concern. He mentioned to Bailey that if the warden didn't show up, they could try it Thursday when the new warden made his tour of the plant.

"He'll show," the bank robber promised.

The teams completed four innings. It was ten o'clock.

Warden Prather finished signing the final papers left on his desk by his secretary the day before. He slowly ripped off the month of May on his desk calendar so Warden Simpson could start off with the proper date, Thursday, June 1, 1933. He stood up, carefully placed the chair into the desk well, and walked to the barber shop. A few moments later, the balding warden thanked the barbers and headed back to his office. Frank Sawyer, anxious to join his friends in the recreation yard, extracted a safety-razor blade from under the counter where he had hidden it for more than six months, pulled shut the shop door, and walked briskly to the ball diamond.

When Prather returned to his office, Joe Lyons, a reporter for the Leavenworth *Times*, and James C. Davis, a Leavenworth undertaker, were waiting. The pair had driven to the prison in Davis's sixteen-cylinder Cadillac with chauffeur John Bradley at the wheel. Lyons had heard rumors about a suspected break and wanted to check with the warden.

"Nothing to it, boys," the warden assured his visitors, who promptly left. It was 10:15. Lyons would miss the greatest story of his career by less than twenty minutes.

At that very moment, Alex Davis wheeled the big Dodge touring car belonging to the Woodson family out of the prison garage. Davis, a black, was a trusty due to be released shortly. He had been given the job of driving the family autos to their owners each morning. It was 10:25 when he pulled into the Woodson driveway and honked. Young Virginia came running down the walk.

"Hi, Alex," the young girl exclaimed. "I get to drive you back today, momma said." She scooted behind the wheel of the six-passenger car, put it into reverse gear, and eased it into the gravel roadway.

"Miss Virginia, the gauge shows the tank's about empty," Davis mentioned. "You'd better fill up before you come back."

Memorial Day was special for Joe Greenrood. As steward at the prison, it was his job to plan and produce the meals. Holidays were always a challenge and Greenrood conjured up extras for the menu. With the two American Legion junior baseball teams as guests, he prepared minced chicken on toast, mashed potatoes and cream gravy, buttered fresh peas and creamed asparagus, cocoanut layer cake and strawberries and cream. Everything was from the prison farm.

After the morning game, the Leavenworth team would dine in a special room set aside for visiting dignitaries, and following the second game in the afternoon, the Topeka youngsters would be feted. Greenrood was particularly pleased since he had been notified two days earlier that Governor Landon was retaining him as steward. He busied himself preparing the table, placing two vases of poppies at a miniature Memorial Day shrine. Greenrood was proud of his World War I army service and draped red, white, and blue bunting around the table. A hand-painted inscription hung above the poppies. It read:

> Can We Forget? Will We Forget?
> In Flanders fields where crimson poppies grow
> And little white crosses stand row on row.

Between the vases was a tiny hand-carved coffin bearing the inscription: "My Buddy." Clyde Paine, a convict whose wood carving had attracted national attention, made the miniature casket especially for the occasion. Greenrood glanced at his wristwatch as he finished the table decorations. It was 10:30.

Milan Wood carefully guided the blue Willys around the curving path of Highway 5. His wife sat beside him viewing the green fields along the Kaw River as the car passed through Wolcott. Soon the highway led past the state women's industrial prison and Wood turned to the back seat.

"Better be good or you'll wind up in there," he joshed. Louise and her friend, Clarice Wears, also seventeen, giggled at the prospect. At Louise's request, Clarice had joined the Wood family since she was alone for the holiday. Her parents were divorced and living in Texas. The young girl lived with an aunt two blocks from the Wood home while completing her studies at the Wyandotte high school. Both Louise and Clarice were to graduate within a week.

Wood glanced at his watch. It was 10:30. Perhaps he shouldn't have taken time to show the family the Memorial Day parade on Minnesota Avenue before starting the journey to Wadsworth, he mused to himself. Just ahead he could see the outline of the state prison and the farm that spread from the walls to the highway. He slowed the car as Highway 5 began a series of dips and turns. Milan Wood had no way of knowing that in five minutes the most frightening time of his life would begin.

The prison twine plant, where Bailey and Davis were assigned, stood north of the baseball diamond. The civilian plant foreman, sixty-nine-year-old Charley Lindsey, and Fred "Red" Ackerson, a guard, were both on duty despite the holiday. They decide to watch the ball game. Next to the twine plant was a small stone building used by the inmates for handicraft work in their spare time. The two men pulled up chairs by the smaller building, which was closer to the diamond and offered a better view of the action. A guard, John Laws, walked by, which prompted Lindsey to ask Ackerson about an argument the two guards had the day before.

"Oh, John is all right once he cools down," Ackerson replied. "The cons all hate his guts and he's real tough on them, but he never gave me any trouble before. He was cracking down on one of my men and when I questioned him about it, he tried to show me up to the deputy warden. We got it straightened out."

Laws took a position behind the backstop near a continually bubbling water fountain used by players and spectators alike.

Atop the twine plant in the special bleachers provided for officers and their families, John Stewart, a fireman in the coal mines, and J. N. Van Meter, a mining "pit boss," were watching the game with their sons, Jack and Rex Stewart, and eight-year-old Jack Van Meter. When the Leavenworth nine took a 2–1 lead in the fifth inning, the boys let out a whoop.

It was 10:35 when the bulky figure of Warden Prather emerged from the administration building. Underhill was the first to spot him.

"Here comes the bastard now," he muttered. Bailey, Clark, Brady, and Sawyer slowly turned, but Davis fixed his cold eyes on Laws. Davis had a score to settle with the belligerent guard. Davis began sidling toward the backstop where Laws was intently watching the game.

Prather walked up beside Laws and asked about the game. Swiftly, the plotters circled the backstop, surrounding Prather and Laws. In a flash, Clark whipped the wire noose around the beefy neck of the warden. Bailey slammed a gun in Prather's ribs and Underhill did the same to Laws. Davis moved next to the chicken-wire screen where Bill Musselman, the prison recreation director, was also watching the game.

Just then a tremendous roar came from the stands. A Topeka player smacked a long drive that cleared the high wall in left field, tying the score. This kept the attention of the guards and spectators from the drama unfolding behind the screen.

The warden began to struggle with the garrote.

"You're getting that too tight," he yelled.

"You got us in here pretty tight, warden," Clark retorted.

Davis jabbed his gun into Musselman's back. The recreation officer turned to face his tormenter. "Don't move or I'll blow you apart," Davis warned. When Musselman started to raise his hands, the convict told him to keep his arms down. He motioned him to join the group beside the throttled warden.

Guard John Sherman was next to feel a jab in the back. He turned to face Sawyer, who had Clark's knife in his hand. Sherman could feel blood oozing from a wound in his back. He joined the ever-increasing knot behind the backstop.

Clark turned the garrote over to Underhill and ran to the hay wagon. He was stunned to see a heavy chain locked around the wheel. Brady, who had gone to the kitchen for the ladder, returned to report someone had moved it. Both realized the only escape now was through the iron door in center field.

Lindsey and Ackerson were quick to notice the activity behind home plate. They slid behind the door of the hobby shop, but Bailey saw the movement and sent Brady to retrieve them. On the field, Coach Meeker, a former guard at the prison, became aware something was amiss. He spotted the warden's predicament. He felt his young players were in no immediate danger, so let the game continue while he attempted to notify a guard. When he saw the group behind the backstop begin to move down the third-base line, he yelled for the players to come in off the field.

The six convicts ordered the unwieldy number of hostages down the third-base line toward Tower 3½. Another guard, Bentley Clark, walked around the corner of the hospital unaware of the circumstances. Brady told him to join the collection of officers. As the incongruous gang moved down the foul line, W. D. Powell, the scorekeeper, wondered why the players were suddenly leaving the field. In the stands, the convicts had discovered the developments near the water fountain. They stood en masse to get a better view. Suddenly, Powell felt his folding chair fly out from under him. As the group walked by, Davis had booted the camp stool and sent the old man sprawling.

"You come along, too," the wiry Oklahoman instructed Powell, who showed considerable sprightliness getting to his feet.

When the group headed toward the outfield, Van Meter and Stewart hustled their sons and the other spectators atop the twine plant into the building. The ball players were pocketed between the twine plant and the engineering building in the event of gunplay. Coach Meeker saw they were safe, then dashed to the warden's office where he attempted to telephone outside for help. Unbelievably, both phones were dead.

Meeker then ran across the hall to the record clerk's office. Four convicts were visiting with a member of the clerk's staff. When Meeker breathlessly told what was happening in the yard, one of the convicts volunteered to call the sheriff's office. The line was busy! Meeker grabbed the phone and called the Fort Leavenworth military police, who promised to block a nearby bridge to Missouri and all roads to the north of the city of Leavenworth. A military search plane was sent aloft to help spot the fleeing convicts.

When the gaggle reached the wall, directly under Tower 3½, Underhill began to shout orders.

"Tell that guard to toss down his guns," he told the warden. Prather, his fear of Underhill evident, quickly passed along the order. Guard Pete Kley tossed down a rifle, which Bailey added to his armament, and two pistols, which were quickly passed to Clark and Sawyer.

At this point, five inmates ran from the stands and asked Underhill if they could join in the break.

Underhill, with a grandiose gesture interpreted by some as inviting all the convicts to come along, waved his left arm high in the air. The five crowded in. They were Sonny Payton, Billie Woods, Kenneth Conn, Lew Bechtel, and Cliff Dopson, doing time for crimes ranging from car theft to murder.

The convicts next moved the group toward Tower 3 in center field. In the tower, Guard Al Courtney, serving his first day on the job, watched in awe as the group marched toward him. His instructions had been to keep his arms in the event of a break, regardless of the hostage situation. He raised his .30-.30 rifle to the ready.

At that moment, the prison siren, known as "the wildcat," sounded. It was 10:40. Only five minutes had elapsed since the wire was whipped around the warden's neck.

Courtney took careful aim and fired a shot into the ground in front of the approaching mob.

"Stop firing," the warden yelled. "Throw down your guns."

Courtney hesitated, confused over the conflicting instructions. The heavily perspiring warden motioned for the guard to act. Courtney lobbed the rifle over the side. The wooden stock struck the ground at an angle and splintered. Underhill screamed at the guard.

"You bastard, throw down the rest of them guns and if one more busts, I'll shoot your ass off," he railed.

Courtney carefully tossed down two more guns, which the convicts snatched up quickly.

"Now toss down them keys and make it snappy," Underhill ordered. The wildcat continued to wail and was making everyone jittery. Two miles away at the Lansing cemetery, the Pettijohns and Warrens were preparing to leave, aware the siren meant trouble at the prison.

"We better get moving," Ralph Pettijohn advised. "There's going to be some excitement around here pretty soon." The children were delighted to get started for the planned picnic.

Residents as far away as Leavenworth, seven miles to the north, could hear the shrill wailing of the siren. The town of Lansing at the very gates of the prison became alive, although many residents were still sleeping because of the holiday.

Inside the walls, at the foot of the tower, Underhill tried to jam a key into the iron door, which swung open at impact. It had never been locked, Guard Courtney having forgotten to secure it on his first day on duty. The convicts goaded their hostages up the circular staircase to the tower, where Courtney stood with hands held high above his head.

Clark sized up the tower interior. A coil of rope, used in the winter months to hoist buckets of coal up the outside wall for the stove, lay piled in one corner. Clark hastily tied the rope to a steel stanchion alongside the tower and dropped the loose end over the side. Sawyer tested the line, then lowered himself, hand over hand, to the ground below. Davis, holding a revolver tightly in his right hand, motioned toward Guard Ackerson.

"Down you go," he ordered. The guard hesitated, then began to back along the top of the limestone wall. Davis raised his gun to eye level, pointing it at Ackerson's head.

Bailey grabbed Davis by the arm.

"Leave him be. We got enough hostages with the warden and a couple of guards. We don't need no more," Bailey shouted.

Davis glared at Bailey an instant.

"Then let's take Laws. I got a score to settle with him," he retorted.

"God damn it, we're wasting time. Let's get goin'," Bailey yelled.

Davis then slid down the rope, joining Sawyer on the ground.

Bailey picked up the rope and turned to Ackerson.

"You go tell them people back there if we're followed, we'll shoot the warden," he instructed. Ackerson nodded.

Bailey eased down the rope, a pistol in his belt band and a rifle tucked against his side. Just as he reached the bottom, a shot rang out and Bailey felt a sharp slap above his right knee. He quickly spotted his assailant, whom he recognized as the dairy supervisor, standing near a railroad car on a siding several hundred feet away. Bailey snapped his rifle to his shoulder, but the supervisor apparently had a one-shot rifle, which he tossed to the ground. Bailey lowered his rifle as blood spurted from his wounded knee.

Atop the wall, Underhill released his grip on the warden's noose.

"Okay, warden, it's your turn," the killer ordered, suddenly shoving the 200-pound Prather. Surprisingly agile, the warden snared the line in his hands and slid rapidly to the cinder-covered ground below, friction burning his palms badly. Underhill followed, laughing as the badly shaken warden brushed cinders from his bleeding hands. The two guards, Sherman and Laws, were next down the rope, followed by Brady and, finally, Clark. The five uninvited convicts then scrambled to the ground, leaving Musselman, Ackerson, Bentley Clark, Powell, and Courtney standing on top of the wall. Ackerson quickly reeled in the rope, dropped it over the inside wall and slid to the ground to repeat Bailey's instructions. In his haste, he too burned his hands sliding down the rope.

Meanwhile, Officers Van Meter and Stewart had run to the main gate, commandeered a car, and circled to the spot where the prisoners were going over the wall. Stewart sped down Kansas Avenue, the street paralleling the south prison wall, arriving as the desperadoes hit the ground. He swung the car around the intersection to put Van Meter in position to fire. Brady raised a shotgun to his big shoulder and pulled the trigger. The shot tore through the door on Van Meter's side, passed above the officer's lap, and ripped into Stewart's left wrist. Stewart gunned the accelerator to move out of position behind the southeast corner. Four more officers arrived at this time and took refuge behind a garage. Brady peered around the corner, fired two more rounds that peppered the side of a house on the southwest corner of the intersection. He then retreated out of sight.

Meanwhile, Underhill spotted the Woodson car parked at the gasoline pump about seventy-five yards away.

"Come on, gang, here's a car," he yelled, and ran toward the Dodge. Trusty Davis saw the oncoming convicts.

"Run, Miss Virginia, run," he cried, grabbing the young girl by the arm. As she fled toward the garage, the black convict shielded her with his body. The exchange between Brady and the officers caused the pair to believe the shots were being fired at them as they sped to the sanctuary of the building.

While Davis, Sawyer, and Underhill raced to the car, Clark half-carried the crippled Bailey. Brady made sure the warden and the two hostage guards came along. Bailey, Clark, and Underhill got in the back seat, along with Prather, while Brady slipped behind the wheel. Sawyer and Davis sat in the front. The two guards were stationed on either running board.

Payton, Conn, Woods, Bechtel, and Dopson didn't find the luxury of a waiting escape car, so fled into the woods adjacent to the officer housing. Payton carried the shotgun with the shattered stock, the others shared a pistol.

Brady slammed the heavy Dodge in low gear. The officers around the corner were waiting for the convicts to appear and were surprised to see a car hurtling by. They couldn't fire because of the hostages. Van Meter had forced Stewart to return to the prison for treatment of his smashed wrist.

The fleeing convicts roared down Third Street, turned east on Kay, then back south to First Street, where a left turn headed them toward Highway 5 about a mile away. They zipped past the Union Pacific depot, where the station agent, J. L. Connolly, and two buddies, William Morton and J. L. Chandley, were getting ready to go fishing. The three were fixing a slow leak in the right front tire of Chandley's new Chevrolet when the speeding Dodge roared by. They noticed the guards with their familiar leather-billed caps on the running boards.

"Must be after whoever broke out," one of the men commented, aware of trouble because of the screaming siren.

At that moment, there was a crashing in the underbrush and five men appeared a few yards west of the station. Connolly looked up to see a shotgun pointed at him.

"Where are the keys to that car?" Alva Payton demanded.

"Inside, I guess," Connolly lied, motioning toward the station.

Chandley and Morton decided to run and took off down the tracks. Payton raised the shotgun and pulled the trigger. At that precise moment, Chandley tripped over one of the ties and sprawled to the ground, unhurt.

"My God, Sonny, you hit him," one of the convicts cried. "Let's get outta here."

The five men ran down the tracks to First Street. A coupe containing a man and woman topped the hill. The escapees surrounded the vehicle and piled in, forcing the occupants to stand beside the road. The convicts raced toward Highway 5. A blue Willys containing a man, woman, and two girls was approaching.

"Boys, we need a bigger car," Payton announced. "Here comes one we can use." He pulled the coupe crossways in the road.

Milan Wood had no choice but to brake his new Willys to a halt. Instantly he recognized the denim garb of the convicts and surmised the speeding Dodge he'd just seen seconds before with the guards on the running boards was seeking the five men surrounding his car.

The Dodge responded easily to Brady's strong touch despite the passenger load. A mile south of the point the

Dodge passed a Willys going the other direction, Bailey spotted a graveled road.

"Turn here, Bob," Bailey ordered. "If we can get west of 73, there's a bridge across the Kaw that likely won't be guarded if we get there soon enough."

The Dodge was due south of the prison, backtracking westward. Suddenly, the motor began to sputter.

"Christ, we're out of gas," Brady yelled, glancing at the fuel gauge for the first time. He remembered the Dodge was beside the garage gasoline pumps when it was commandeered.

The car gasped and jerked until it came to the intersection of the gravel road and the main highway. Brady stopped the car in the middle of the slab. Seconds later, a blue Chevrolet drove into sight. The driver, spotting the caps of the guards, slowed the car to a stop a few feet behind the stalled Dodge.

Jim Clark, carrying a repeating rifle, approached the Chevrolet.

"We need your car. Get out," he ordered.

Ralph Pettijohn stared in disbelief. For the first time he realized the car was in command of convicts and the guards he saw were hostages. The Warrens and Pettijohns quickly evacuated the car, all except five-year-old Lonnie Warren. Nothing was going to delay his picnic. He steadfastly refused to budge. His mother jerked him from the back seat as Clark sat down in the front seat.

"We aren't going to hurt your car," Clark told Pettijohn. "We just want to drive it a ways and leave it where it'll be found. If there's anything in it you need, better take it out."

Pettijohn reached into the front seat and retrieved his wallet and the family Bible, lying on the seat. He then pulled the Chevy's maintenance book out of the glove compartment.

Brady again took the wheel. The others piled into the Chevy with the identical arrangement they had in the deserted Dodge. Bailey's knee was bleeding profusely and he was growing weak. Prather, pale and shaken, stared absently, pondering his fate, Bailey on his left and the ebullient Underhill, excitedly waving a revolver, on his right. The two guards hung tenaciously to the running boards.

Standing on Highway 5, Milan Wood watched in horror as his crippled wife, daughter, her young friend, and the five convicts disappeared down the road. He futilely turned for aid and was stunned to see a car parked atop the hill less than a hundred yards away. Half a dozen armed guards were watching.

He rushed to the men, who were re-entering their car.

"Why didn't you do something?" Wood demanded to know.

"Mister, we couldn't fire into that bunch without hitting those women folk," one of the officers replied. The car sped off in pursuit of the escaping criminals. Wood hailed a passing motorist and was taken into Lansing, where he waited for word about his missing loved ones.

In the Willys, Sonny Payton kept a firm grip on the steering wheel. Highway 5's crooked route offered dangerous turns and narrow bridges. He glanced at the white-faced woman seated between him and Conn.

"Look, lady, we ain't gonna hurt you none," he told the frightened Mrs. Wood. "We just got out of Lansing, and as soon as we get where we're going, we'll let you out."

Bechtel, Dopson, and Woods—all small men, five foot six and 120 pounds at most—had crowded into the back of the car with Louise and her friend. Conn turned around in the front seat and tried to chat with the girls, but they were too terrified to answer.

Payton, from Labette County, was a lot older than his twenty-two years. He'd led a rugged life and was serving twenty-years-to-life for murder. Kenneth Conn, twenty-one, a murderer from Pratt, Kansas, had been his prison buddy. He barely knew the others—Billie Woods, twenty-two, a car thief sentenced from Dodge City; Cliff Dopson, nineteen, a St. Louis kid sent up from Columbus, Kansas, for robbery; and Lewis Bechtel, twenty-eight, a cowboy from Idaho, army deserter, and highway robber sent up from Sharon Springs.

Payton took a cat road near the Kaw River community of Wolcott. Since their decision to join the break had been impromptu, they had no escape plan, and Bechtel suggested they stop and concoct one. Payton halted the Willys in a heavily wooded area. He and Woods stayed in the car to guard the women, while the others got out to discuss the matter. It was decided the Cookson Hills of Oklahoma offered the best sanctuary. The group would, of course, run the cat roads most of the way.

Thus, all eleven men involved in the largest prison break in the state's history were heading for the same objective—the Cookson Hills.

# The Chase

# 10

Law officials immediately guessed the fleeing convicts would head toward the Cooksons. In small towns south of Lansing, policemen were instructed to keep lookouts for the escapees. Roadblocks were set up along both sections of Highway 73, the most direct roads south to the Oklahoma line. (Today, 73E is U.S. 69, 73W is U.S. 59.) To the east, on the Missouri side, the Jackson County sheriff's patrol set up a block at the state line.

The confiscated Chevrolet driven by Brady purred quietly along 73E. Bailey, despite his agonizing pain, told his companions to hit the bumpy cat roads immediately.

Prather, the noose still around his neck, tried to visit with his kidnappers. He asked Underhill about his mother, for whom the convict had been allowed to pass the hat.

"I'm gonna kill that doctor," Underhill growled. "He didn't set the bone right." Prather, realizing his inquiry had only nettled the desperado, fell silent. Underhill, agitated and excited, still held a .45 revolver, shifting it from one hand to the other. Suddenly, the gun discharged. The bullet screamed past Bailey's ear and shattered the back window of the sedan. Despite his weakening condition, Bailey cursed Underhill and warned him to be more careful.

Avoiding Bonner Springs, where they thought the well-traveled bridge would probably be watched, they continued west, picked up Kansas 32, and, at Linwood, crossed the Kaw. The bridge was unguarded. Once across the river, Brady suggested a stop for gasoline. They pulled into the Rothberger station in Eudora. John Rothberger, noting the guns, asked if they were going hunting.

"Yeah," Brady smiled. "Know any good places around here?"

Rothberger indicated he wasn't much of a hunter, took a dollar for five gallons of gasoline, and the conversation ended.

Brady picked up 73W north of Ottawa. Just before reaching the Franklin County seat, a patrol car filled with armed officers approached from the south. The convicts pulled off the road, ordering the hostages to take cover in the ditch. About a hundred yards away, the approaching patrol car came to a stop. The occupants huddled for a moment, looking toward the convicts, who had taken battle positions. The officers got back into their car, turned around, and drove away, obviously deciding there would be a better time to jump the escapees. The convicts resumed their journey unmolested.

Underhill began to question Bailey's demands to get back on the cat roads. He argued they could make the Cooksons in two hours by sticking to 73W. North of Parsons, Bailey won out and Brady entered a side road.

The second group of convicts, at their brief roadside conference, had decided to hide during the day at some isolated farmhouse and then go on to the Cooksons. They returned to the car. Dopson ordered Miss Wears to sit on his lap as the journey resumed.

"You can shoot me if you want to, but I won't sit on your lap," she defiantly said. An embarrassing silence followed with no one seeming to know what to do. Miss Wears agreed to sit on Louise Wood's lap and the trip continued.

Payton, searching for a farmhouse, came to Kansas 32, where he turned west. A short distance later, he turned off on a dirt road leading south. The convicts were now about two and a half miles east of Edwardsville on County Road OK where Mr. and Mrs. Henry McGee made their home.

Alpha McGee had set the noon table for herself and for her husband, their sister-in-law, Louetta McGee, and Louetta's two children, all working in the potato fields close by. She was puttering in her flower garden when the convicts drove up. It was about 11:15 a.m.

Bechtel and Woods stepped from the Willys.

"Lady, we'll pay you for lunch and we'd like to stay here for the afternoon," Bechtel, brandishing a pistol, told the farm woman. She was so terrified she couldn't answer.

The convicts tromped into the farmhouse, noticing the five place settings.

"Looks like somebody'll be here for lunch," Conn said. "We better clear out."

Payton, looking around the room, spotted McGee's shotgun in the corner.

"Yeah, we'd better get moving," Payton agreed, picking up the gun. Mrs. McGee, who never left her flower garden, watched as the intruders re-entered their car.

Henry McGee, working in his field, could see the strange car in his driveway. It was about time to knock off for lunch, anyway, so he and his nephews and sister-in-law headed toward the house. They saw the denim-clad convicts re-enter the car, then back around in the driveway. The rear wheels became mired in mud. As Payton gunned the engine, the wheels suddenly caught on dry ground, and the car lurched backward. Miss Wood was thrown forward and bumped Bechtel, still holding a pistol. The impact caused him to squeeze the trigger and the gun exploded. The bullet smashed the rear window of the car. Everyone was visibly shaken by the unexpected blast.

The car was still stuck, so Payton ordered everyone out to push. Once it was free, Payton headed back to the main highway, where he turned west. Passing through Edwardsville and Bonner Springs, the car turned south at the De Soto bridge to cross the Kaw River. Unbelievably, there were no guards at the busy bridge. Payton doubled back east toward Kansas City, passing well north of Olathe. Near Lenexa, Payton noted the car's tank running low.

"Hey, we need some gas. Anybody got any money?"

Since the five had not planned on being involved in a break, each had left whatever money he had in his cell during the ballgame.

"Let's hit a filling station," Conn suggested.

"Hell, no, that's too dangerous as hot as we are," Bechtel decided.

"Girls, you got any money in your purses? Let's see," he ordered. Grabbing Miss Wears's purse, he dug out seventy cents.

After getting three and a half gallons of gasoline, Payton headed the Willys south on 73E, driving through the little towns of Trading Post and Pleasanton, holding the speed to fifty miles per hour so as not to attract undue attention.

Because the Wood family had watched the early-morning Memorial Day parade before leaving for the cemetery, the girls had brought along light spring coats. Woods and Dopson, because of their slight builds, put the coats around their shoulders to give the impression there were five women in the auto. There was much light-hearted chiding by their companions as the car moved easily along the highway.

Warden Prather could feel the mounting tension as the Chevrolet neared the Oklahoma line. The noose had chafed his neck raw and he asked if it could be removed. Underhill untied the noose and tossed it out the car window. While rubbing his sore neck, Prather turned the diamond on his ring to the inside of his finger. The sharp-eyed Bailey, despite his weakened condition, noticed the warden's gesture.

"Hell, warden, we ain't gonna take your ring," he laughed. Prather didn't return the smile.

Davis looked back at Prather from the front seat.

"You tell that bastard Frank O'Brien we're gonna bump him off for giving us that bum rap. We didn't do that Fort Scott job."

Prather knew Davis was referring to the Bourbon County attorney who had prosecuted Clark, Davis, and Sawyer in the bank-robbery trial.

"I'll tell him," Prather breathed, the first indication he'd had that the kidnappers might not kill him.

Suddenly, the car began to overheat. Brady, peering into the rearview mirror, had been watching a car following for the past few minutes. In the car behind were Mr. and Mrs. Ed Clum, their nine-year-old son, LeRoy, and Mr. and Mrs. Parker Hall. Clum had been driving to the Galesburg cemetery when they first spotted an approaching car with men on the running boards.

"Aren't those prison guards?" Mrs. Hall asked. She remarked that it was possibly the escape car she'd heard about on the radio that morning.

"Well, let's see if it is," the adventurous Clum said, turning his car around to follow the Cheverolet. After a few minutes, the lead car stopped. Clum halted his machine a short distance behind. Three men and the guards alighted from the Chevrolet and approached on foot.

"Unload," one man said, motioning with a shotgun. The Clums and Halls quickly evacuated the Durant touring car.

"Why are you following us?" the man with the shotgun asked.

"We thought you were someone we knew," Clum lied.

"Well, you damn sure followed the wrong bunch."

"I realize my mistake, now," Clum stated.

The gunman searched Clum, took $2.35 from his pockets.

"Now, get in that car with us," he was ordered.

Clum started to protest, but when he saw two of the convicts get into his car, he pleaded with them to treat the women and the boy kindly.

"Don't worry. We'll treat them alright."

Hall got in behind the Durant's steering wheel. Frank Sawyer sat between the two women in the back seat, Clark sat in the front seat alongside the boy, who was crying. Clum sat in the front seat of the Chevy, Prather, Bailey, and Underhill remaining in the back seat and Brady at the wheel. Guards Laws and Sherman again were ordered to the running boards of the Chevy, which now had cooled sufficiently for Brady to start it. Hall followed in the Durant.

Bailey, his knee still oozing blood through a grimy bandage of denim strips from his pants leg, asked Clum if he had any cigarettes. He produced a pack of Chesterfields, each man taking one except Prather, who had remained mute during this entire episode.

"Don't drive too fast," Clum warned Brady. "My car is old and won't stand it." He tried to appear at ease and attempted to be jovial with the convicts.

As the two cars jolted down the farm road, heading toward the main highway, Sawyer struck up a conversation with the ladies.

"You know, five more guys that broke out with us are somewhere in Kansas. You sure are lucky you didn't run into them."

"Yes, we heard on the radio this morning before we left

for the cemetery," Mrs. Hall responded. "I think we should have a souvenir of this adventure," she added.

"Here's your souvenir, lady," Sawyer said, handing her a cigarette lighter. He gave Mrs. Clum a photograph of a girl, but didn't identify her.

East of Parsons, they had to stop when the Chevy overheated again. Hall noted the Durant was almost out of gas. He mentioned the fact to the convicts, who decided it was time to let their newest hostages have their car back.

"Drive as far as you can," Bailey told Hall. "If you don't squawk about anything, everything will be pretty." The Halls and Clums indicated they'd be silent about the whole thing.

"We might even send you some money some day," Bailey added with a grin. "By the way, where's the nearest filling station?"

Clum, who worked for a creamery in the area, said there wasn't one near. When the Chevy cooled, the convicts got back in and headed south. Clum drove the Durant to the first farm house to notify law officers. No one was home, as was the case at a second home. Finally, he came to a barbecue stand, "The House That Jack Built," and was able to call the Parsons police.

As the convicts continued toward the safety of the Cooksons, Sawyer produced a pint of whiskey he'd found in the Clum car. Each man took a nip and the whiskey seemed to revive Bailey, whose knee was bleeding less by this time.

Prather again tried to placate his captors.

"You boys sure pulled a clever job," he remarked. "We had a tip two weeks ago you were smuggling in guns, and we searched every sisal bale in the place."

Bailey laughed. "Not the right ones."

"Our tip must have been wrong," the warden admitted.

Underhill became infuriated. "What son of a bitch ratted on us? Who gave you the tip?"

The warden said he didn't know, although he did. (Stanton Zook, an inmate from Parsons, was paroled by the governor for giving Prather the tip. Zook and Underhill had become bitter enemies behind the walls, and Zook, fearful Underhill would kill him, gave away the plot. But it was Underhill's earlier plot Zook referred to, not knowing about the one Clark and Brady were planning.)

In the meantime, the other escapees had found a shady lane south of Pleasanton, where they decided to hide the remainder of the day. "We'll park here until dark, then find some place to stay," Bechtel declared, as the convicts and their hostages piled out of the cramped quarters.

"Damn, I'm sure hungry," Billie Woods remarked, stretching his weary muscles after the two-hour ride. "When we gonna get some grub?"

"We'll wait until after dark," Bechtel said, again.

After allowing the women to stretch for a while, Bechtel forced them back into the car. The prisoners lolled in the shade, recounting tales of the past and smoking hand-rolled cigarettes.

As dusk fell, Conn noticed a farm boy coming down the road. The youngster, whistling loudly, never noticed the parked car as he cut through a pasture. The convicts guessed there was a farmhouse nearby.

"Let's find where that kid lives and get some food," Payton suggested.

"Tie up the girls and let's go," Bechtel ordered. The women protested they, too, were hungry, so Dopson and Woods remained as guards while the other three went off in search of food and lodging for the night.

Memorial Day ended like any other day on the William New farm. Tired from a long day of routine chores, Bill New put out the flaming wick of the kerosene lamp and settled into the billowy feather bed. Beside him, his wife had retired earlier, exhausted from caring for eight-een-month-old Carrie Geraldine. In the other bedroom, young Loren Morrell, the farm hand back from his early-evening hike, also was asleep.

Dusk was settling over the southern Kansas farmlands when the Pettijohn Chevrolet neared the border. Brady held the wheel steady as the car bumped along a cat road due south of the little town of Altamont. Ahead was Oklahoma.

Within two miles after crossing the border, a tire blew out. The cursing convicts piled out to repair it. Bailey and the warden sat beside the road in the gathering darkness while Clark and Sawyer labored over the patching job. Underhill suddenly pulled out his pistol and ordered Sherman and Laws to walk to a patch of woods nearby. The guards looked at each other apprehensively.

Bailey, revived after his knee quit bleeding, yelled at Underhill.

"Listen, you put that thing away," Bailey ordered, motioning toward Underhill's gun. "No sir, there ain't no killin' gonna come off here. You make one move and I'll christen you."

Underhill, although he was fearless and had a deep dislike for Bailey, nevertheless respected the older man. He hesitated, then jammed the revolver in his waist band.

"All right, if that's the way you want it."

He strode back to the car.

The tire repaired, the group re-entered the car. A few miles further, Bailey ordered the car stopped near a rusty steel bridge.

"Warden, we're gonna let you out here. You got any money?"

The warden indicated he had eleven cents in pocket change.

"What a cheap lot," Underhill bellowed. "Here, take a

buck and buy some smokes—if you ever get back to civilization."

Prather and the two guards watched with great relief as
the car's red tail lights disappeared in the dark. They could
hardly believe their good luck. They were alive and unharmed and free to make their way back to "civilization,"
which, despite Underhill's sneering remark, was not that
far away. They started walking.

Lawmen in three states were hard at work seeking
the two groups. Reports filtered in from all directions
about the fleeing desperadoes. Jess Weatherby, a filling-
station operator midway between Picher and Miami, Oklahoma, was held up by five men. Since it was dark, the
sixth, he reasoned, could have remained in the car, unseen. Sheriff Dee Watters of Ottawa County, Oklahoma,
correctly guessed both gangs' destination as the Cooksons
and believed Bailey, because of his wound, had been taken
to a hideout. He based his theory on Weatherby reporting
only five men.

"Underhill knows this country like a book and they are
doing some fancy backtracking," the sheriff announced.
Actually, it was Clark who was steering them through the
area.

The convicts were "seen" at Foraker in the Osage Hills,
not far from the Cooksons. This prompted speculation they
were heading for the Grammar ranch, twelve miles east of
Ponca City. Henry Grammar, a noted badman, had been
killed in an auto accident ten years before and it was said
his widow, Maggie, hid some of her late husband's outlaw
buddies on the ranch from time to time. The Grammar
theory was supported by the fact Sawyer had been with
Al Spencer, another Osage Hills all-around badman, and
knew the area.

Sheriff Bob LaFollette of Washington County, Arkansas,
felt at least one of the two carloads might stray into his

territory. He warned his deputies to watch for any strange cars with Kansas plates.

Back at Lansing, Mrs. Prather kept a vigil in her husband's office. R. D. Payne, the warden's secretary, propped his feet on the warden's desk, pushed his Panama hat to the back of his head, and looked at the clock on the wall. It had been eight hours since any word of the warden or his captors had been heard.

A pounding noise awakened Bill New with a start. He had just dozed off and was slightly groggy as he made his way to the upstairs bedroom window. On the porch below he could make out the forms of three men.

"What do you want?" New inquired.

"Come on down and let us in," one of the figures commanded. Mrs. New joined her husband.

"We'd better see what they want, Bill," she said.

New stepped into his overalls and descended the steps, carrying a freshly lighted coal-oil lamp. The wall clock revealed it was 8:30 p.m.

He unlatched the door. The three men strode forward.

The shortest of the three spoke, looking past New to his wife, standing midway on the stairway.

"Everybody be quiet. Don't make any fuss and everything will be okay."

New then noticed each man carried a firearm.

The short man spoke again, pointing toward Mrs. New.

"You go fix supper for eight."

The leader turned to his two companions.

"You guys go get the others. I'll stay here."

Mrs. New said she needed some kindling and firewood for the cookstove.

"Hey, you guys, bring some wood in before you go," the leader instructed.

Presently, the pair returned with armloads of firewood

from a pile New had stacked on the back porch. Then, they went out.

The short man took a seat in the front room, his arm accidentally brushing a crocheted antimacassar to the floor.

"My name's Lew Bechtel. We just got out of the pen at Lansing and we're going to stay here awhile. We ain't gonna hurt nobody, so just take it easy."

A few minutes later, the door swung open and the other escapees and the three women hostages straggled in. Mrs. Wood had to be aided to a sofa, where she immediately stretched out. The two girls sat together in an overstuffed chair.

Mrs. New busied herself in the kitchen, then entered the room where the convicts and their hostages were resting.

"I can't kill a chicken this time of night," she announced, "but I can make some bacon and eggs."

"That's fine with me," Bechtel said. The other convicts nodded assent.

Soon the food was ready and the five convicts and their hostages gathered around the New's oak dining table. The men ate voraciously, but the girls picked at their food and Mrs. Wood was unable to eat anything. She returned to the sofa while the others remained at the table.

Following the meal, Mrs. New went to her bedroom to check on Carrie Geraldine.

"She's been fretting all day," she explained. Oddly enough, the fifteen-year-old farm hand continued to sleep.

Prather, Sherman, and Laws decided to walk east, the direction the convicts took. The desolate hills revealed no lights indicating a farm home, and after three miles of steady plodding, the lawmen became footsore. Sherman once thought he saw a car's lights ahead, going north, which would indicate a crossroads. Soon they arrived at a general store at an intersection called Pyramid Corners, but the store had closed at sundown. The weary trio considered breaking in but saw no lines to indicate the store had a telephone. They trudged on.

About midnight, they came across a home at the edge of the little town of Welch, ten miles south of the Kansas border. Prather roused the occupants and called the prison. Payne answered the phone.

"Hello, Payne, this is the warden."

Payne yelled, "He's safe. He's safe." Into the phone, he said, "My God, man, where are you? Are you all right?"

"I'm alright and so are Laws and Sherman," the warden answered. "They threatened to kill us, but they didn't. We'll get a ride back as soon as we can. Let me talk to my wife."

Mrs. Prather grabbed the phone. Her vigil had lasted thirteen hours.

"Can't you come home by plane?" she asked.

"I'll be home as soon as possible, dear," the warden responded.

At the New farm home, everyone was settling down for the night. The exhausted girls and Mrs. Wood dropped off to sleep immediately, while the News returned to their second-floor bedroom. The escapees stretched out on the floor. Payton, after cutting the telephone wires, found a spot near the open door. A gentle breeze cooled the night.

# The Cooksons

# 11

Bob Brady could make out the initial outline of the Cookson Hills ahead. Steering the blue Chevrolet easily with one big hand, Brady unerringly rolled a cigarette with his free hand. As the headlights of the car groped for the roadway, he sucked deeply on the cigarette.

"Where in the hell are we?" he asked no one in particular.

Clark, who knew the Cooksons better than the others, indicated they were near Salina. Minutes later, the car sped through the tiny community and soon passed through Rose, then the town named Kansas.

"We'll be at Marion Pike's place in less than an hour," Clark stated. "Hang on, Harve. We'll get your knee fixed up soon. Marion knows somebody who can doctor it."

Pike, a half-breed Cherokee, had befriended many men on the run before, including Clark when he fled the prison camp in 1932.

The Cooksons, like the Osage Hills and the Cherokee

117

Hills of northeastern Oklahoma, were filled with ravines, canyons, gullies, and thick forests. The natives, mostly Cherokee Indians, eked out a living fishing and hunting. They were among the most poverty-stricken people in the nation. For decades, the area had been a refuge for outlaws. Often lawmen venturing into the hills were never seen again. Posses long ago had ceased seeking quarries amidst the heavy brush, box canyons, and uncooperative residents.

The Cooksons had no distinct boundaries. Often a resident claimed he lived in the Cooksons while a neighbor across the road identified the area as the Salisaw Hills or the Cherokee Hills. To the north, in Craig County, was the Blue Canyon, which geographically launched the hill country. The canyon, which parallels the course of Big Creek, is composed of a series of gulches, one deeper than the next, some dropping seventy-five feet from the prairie land. This was where the Belle Starr gang made its headquarters prior to the turn of the century. The Poe-Hart gang, composed of Oscar Poe and twin brothers Bill and George Hart, chose this spot to launch their forays against the banks and stores of southern Kansas. When Al Spencer spent six years robbing and hijacking, he used Blue Canyon as his den. The Matt and George Kimes gang and the Jarrett brothers also hid successfully in its grottoes.

The only partially successful foray by lawmen into the canyon was in 1932 when fifteen men chased the Jake Fleagle gang into the wild country. They returned with two gang members, Frank Lane and Fred Cody. After that, many of the outlaws moved to the Osage Hills, around the town of Wynona. Then, when Spencer was killed there, the outlaw element sought safety to the southeast—the Cooksons.

As the fleeing Chevrolet neared Pike's place, the spirits of the escapees soared. Underhill, again toying with a re-

volver, chattered like a chipmunk. Even Bailey, whose
knee throbbed with every turn of the car's wheel, felt
stronger. Clark, alert to see that Brady made the proper
turn, stared at the jiggling beams of light on the road.

Suddenly, Brady began to laugh, his big chest shaking.

"There was sure some scared hombres when Wilbur
wanted to take them guards for a little walk," he chortled.

"Shit, yes. I never seen a cop that didn't need killin',"
Underhill grinned, shifting his revolver to his left hand as
he pushed back a shock of brown hair from his forehead.

"That Laws should of got his," Davis said, remembering
his hatred of the tough guard. "He's a lucky bastard."

Bailey, who had undoubtedly saved the lives of the warden and two guards by demanding that Underhill leave
them alone, steered the conversation in another direction.

"How long now, Jim? My knee is killin' me," Bailey
asked.

"When we get to Peggs, we go two miles south and a
mile east and we'll be there," Clark replied.

Thirty minutes later, Clark spotted the light in Pike's
cabin window. Brady eased across a culvert and into the
yard. While Clark and Sawyer went to the door, the others
lifted Bailey from the back seat.

"Put him on the cot," Clark instructed, pointing toward
a quilt-covered bed on the screened-in porch.

Pike recognized Clark instantly and beckoned the visitors in. Bailey, moaning slightly, was lowered to the cot.
The others went inside.

"Marion, can you get a doc out here? Old Man Bailey's
pretty banged up," Clark asked his Indian friend.

Pike, poking at the fire in the cookstove, knowing his
visitors were hungry, had heard nothing about the break.

"There's a doctor in Locust Grove I can get out here
tomorrow," Pike responded, cracking some eggs in a skillet
for his guests.

The exhausted escapees ate their meal of eggs and bread and then retired for the night.

Sonny Payton was the first to arise at the New farm and began yelling at his companions.

"Let's make some tracks. We can make the Cooksons by noon if we get started," he shouted.

Turning to New, who had come downstairs when he heard the noise, Payton demanded the keys to the farmer's car.

"Billie, there's a storage tank by the barn. Go gas up both cars," Payton said to Woods. "I'll get some of this guy's overalls for us to wear and we can take off." New dug up five pairs of faded overalls for the convicts.

"All right, girls, let's get moving," Payton told the women.

"Why don't you leave us here?" Mrs. Wood asked. "I can't travel any more."

The convicts thought it over. With the telephone line cut and New's car in their possession, they felt no immediate fear of the alarm bring spread. They left the women at the New home.

Woods pulled the New car alongside the porch and Dopson got in. The other escapees got in the Willys. Without a word to the News, they drove off.

New immediately began repairing the telephone line with baling wire. When he got it fixed later that morning, he called the police, and Captain Stanley Beatty of Kansas City, Kansas, drove to the farm and returned the women to their homes. Doctors' examinations revealed the women had not been harmed and had suffered no ill effects from the wild ride. In fact, Mrs. Wood told reporters the convicts had been kind, and she publicly thanked them for their treatment of her and the girls.

North of Fort Scott, the convicts abandoned the New car when it began sputtering badly, and everyone got back into the Willys.

After crossing into Oklahoma, Woods and Dopson, both big-city boys from St. Louis, decided they'd take their chances in their home town rather than the lonely Cooksons.

"Let us out here. We're going to St. Louis," Woods announced. Payton wheeled the Willys to the side of the road.

"Hell, you don't even know where you are."

"We'll find our way," Dopson answered.

"You guys can have those damn hills," Woods added.

As Payton drove away, only Conn bothered to wave.

Woods and Dopson had gotten out southeast of Miami, Oklahoma, at the junction of State Road 10 and a smaller cat road. They began walking east toward Missouri. Traffic was light. At sundown, they decided to bum a meal at a farm house. They spent the night in the farmer's barn.

Meanwhile, Payton, Conn, and Bechtel were running low on gasoline in the Willys. Running the cat roads had consumed much of their fuel and much of the day.

"This car's too hot, Sonny," Bechtel said. "Let's get another one."

Spotting a road sign indicating the town of Jay was a mile away, Bechtel suggested a stop there. It was almost dark when they hit the outskirts, and the little town's two service stations were already closed. They continued south to the junction of state roads near the town of Kansas.

"We gotta get some gas quick," Payton advised. "Let's go on over to Siloam Springs." The Arkansas town, thirteen miles east, seemed the closest place to either steal another car or get refueled.

At the northern outskirts of Siloam Springs, the trio pulled into the farmyard of Cleveland Beatty. After breaking into the barn, Payton jumped the starter on an old car they found there and left the Willys. Less than a mile away, the Beatty car ran out of gas. After considerable cursing, the three men began to walk. A truck approached and they waved their arms frantically but the driver refused to stop. Payton shot his pistol at the truck as it roared past.

Finally, they came across a parked car. Payton attempted to jump the ignition but it was so dark he couldn't find the correct wiring. "Let's push it down to that streetlight so I can see what I'm doing," Payton suggested.

It was almost midnight and Sheriff Bob LaFollette had just completed his rounds when the phone in his office rang.

"Sheriff, this is Mrs. Stout. I just saw three men push my son's car down the street," the voice on the phone said.

"I'll be there right away," LaFollette told the caller.

When he arrived at the residence, there was no evidence of the men or the car. Suddenly, the sheriff's ear caught the sound of a car engine starting. LaFollette saw the Chevrolet coupe a block away, under a streetlight, and recognized it as belonging to Clint Thompson, Mrs. Stout's son. The sheriff leaped into his sedan and gave chase. The coupe sped north, and dust churned high into the night air. LaFollette, who was left-handed, which allowed him to shoot reasonably well while leaning out of the car window, began firing a shotgun at the car's tires. The desperadoes returned the sheriff's fire. LaFollette then realized he wasn't dealing with ordinary car thieves. Attempting to get close enough to fire into the car, LaFollette was accelerating when the Thompson car suddenly turned left and slid around a corner. Before he could slow the patrol car sufficiently, it skidded into a ditch and was disabled.

A resident, attracted by the shooting, saw the sheriff's predicament and telephoned LaFollette's brother, Ivan, who was a deputy sheriff. The brothers searched north of town and discovered the deserted Willys on the Beatty farm. The Kansas plates and items found in the car convinced the LaFollettes the pursued car thieves were some of the escapees from the Kansas prison.

"Ivan, go call Harold Perrine at the newspaper and tell him about this, so he can put it on the wire to Fort Smith," the sheriff instructed his brother. The newspaper wire service was the only news communications outlet at the time. Thus, for the first time law enforcement officers knew the whereabouts of the second band of escapees.

In the meantime, Bechtel had driven west of Siloam Springs about five miles when he decided he'd had enough.

"Boys, I'm going to let you take it," he announced. "I'm heading back to Idaho. You guys can go to the Cooksons if you want, but I'm going back home. This country is horseshit."

Conn decided to remain with Payton and the pair drove off, leaving Bechtel standing alongside the road.

Bechtel looked at the stars and realized just how alone he was. "Ain't like Big Sky country," he mused, looking around for a place to rest for the remainder of the night. He found a pile of brush near a road grader used to repair the roadway. He soon fell fast asleep.

A native of Vanwick, Idaho, where he was born on May 27, 1905, Bechtel was only fifteen when he first got in trouble. He was investigated for burglary in Portland, Oregon, and in Roseburg. He returned to Idaho and was arrested in Cascade for horse stealing. He became Number 1116 at the St. Anthony's Reformatory. Released from the reformatory, he joined the Army and was sent to Camp Washington, Idaho. He became a member of the Third Infantry, got the likeness of an Indian girl tattooed on his shoulder just like his buddies. After a year's service, he deserted. He roamed the Midwest, robbing a filling station or a grocery store on occasion but generally working as a laborer. In Omaha, Nebraska, in October, 1926, he was picked up for vagrancy and discovered to be a deserter. He was sent to the Fort Snelling, Minnesota, stockade for six months. Returned to the Third Infantry, he was reassigned to Company "A", but a change of companies didn't make him like army life any better. He deserted again. In March, 1927, he was picked up for robbing a filling station in Sharon Springs, Kansas, and sentenced for ten to twenty-five years to the reformatory at Hutchinson. He escaped in a matter of weeks.

In February, 1928, Bechtel took a run-down room at 408 West Ninth in Kansas City's downtown area and, despite the cold weather, managed to get a few jobs as a laborer. He and three others who lived in the low-rent area, George Meadows, Albert Tooker, and Victor Halstead, robbed a filling station. They were caught minutes later and tossed in the Kansas City jail. Justice worked swiftly in 1928, and with his record, Bechtel was convicted, sentenced, and began serving a five-year sentence in the Missouri state prison within five days of the robbery. By early 1931, he had earned his discharge on merit time. However, Kansas officials were waiting for him to serve the remainder of his time for the Sharon Springs heist. As an escapee, he was taken to Lansing, where the security was tighter than at the reformatory.

At dawn, in Pike's cabin, Clark awakened his companions.

"We got to hide that car before somebody spots it. They might have a plane flying around looking for us," he warned. They drove to nearby Rattlesnake Canyon, where they covered the car with brush. Pike left soon after for Locust Grove and returned before noon with the doctor. Bailey's knee was badly crusted and bits of denim from his prison uniform were imbedded in the wound. The old doctor swabbed a few of the specks of cloth from the wound, then bandaged it tightly.

Clark gave Pike a twenty-dollar bill to pay the doctor

and buy some cheap clothing in Locust Grove when he returned to the town. By mid-afternoon, the men had changed into seersucker trousers and cotton shirts.

"As soon as the Old Man can travel, we'll light out for Oklahoma City and get him some better treatment or he'll lose that leg," Clark said.

As Bechtel aroused from his night's slumber on the brush pile, dawn brightened the Oklahoma landscape. Delaware County commissioner Earl Coppedge and Floyd Glenn, a county deputy sheriff who worked for the commissioner's office when needed, drove up to the road grader to prepare for the day's work just as Bechtel was stirring nearby. In the early morning light, they failed to notice the convict until he was several hundred yards away, walking from them along a section road crossing Highway 11.

"Who's that fellow?" Coppedge asked Glenn.

"Stranger to me," Glenn replied. "Probably some bum. I'll check him out pretty soon."

By the time the men got the equipment started, Bechtel had reached the Andy Bell farm a mile north of the highway. He asked the elderly Mrs. Bell for breakfast, which she readily prepared. Deputy Glenn walked in the kitchen door without knocking, greeted the Bells, who were seated beside Bechtel at the big kitchen table. Glenn pulled up a chair beside the stranger.

"Howdy. You're a stranger in these parts," Glenn stated.

"Yeah, Johnson's my name. I'm a farm hand on my way to Oregon," Bechtel answered, continuing to eat breakfast.

"I'm a deputy sheriff and I think you'd better come with me into Jay," Glenn announced. He had no gun, but Bechtel offered no resistance. Coppedge, waiting outside in the car, drove the men to Jay, where the escapee was turned over to Undersheriff Okie Kirkwood. Once in jail, Bechtel admitted his identity, and Lansing was notified. It was

Thursday, June 1, and the first of the eleven escapees had been recaptured. Two days later, Bechtel was back on the rock pile.

The morning of June 2, Bailey and the five men with him left Pike's place. They drove to Oklahoma City, where another of Clark's Indian friends, Roy Johnson, would hide them.

Bailey's knee was badly infected, and by the time another doctor was located to treat it, the leg was swollen twice its normal size. Clark contacted some friends of Bailey, who let them borrow money, and then found the wounded man an apartment. He also arranged for a full-time nurse. Davis and Brady, who were both married, began searching for houses to rent. Underhill, Sawyer, and Clark stayed overnight at Johnson's place, then contacted a bootlegger friend of Clark's named Thompson, who agreed to rent them space in his house. But Sawyer and Thompson got in an argument early in the day and the escapees were ordered out of the house. Sawyer, who didn't get along well with Davis and Underhill, decided to split from the group and visit relatives near Corn, Oklahoma. He left afoot. Clark gave him his last fifty cents, then joined Underhill to look for a place to stay. They decided to return to Pike's shack in the Cooksons.

B. K. Blair and Alice Braithwaite drove into the picnic grounds west of Seneca, Missouri, Saturday afternoon, June 3. The young couple had motored from Joplin to enjoy the scenic countryside and find a spot for a picnic. As they spread the tablecloth on the ground, Blair noticed two men walking across a pasture toward them. Blair paid little attention to the approaching men until, about twenty-five yards away, one dropped to his knees and pulled a pistol from his overalls pocket.

"Don't make a move. We're taking your car and you, too," the man said.

The stunned couple was instructed to walk to their car. Blair was ordered into the back seat, Miss Braithwaite in front with the driver. Neither kidnapper spoke for several miles until the driver showed Miss Braithwaite his burned hands.

"My name is Billie Woods," he explained, "and me and my buddy here broke outta the state pen up at Lansing. We burned our hands sliding down a rope over the wall."

He said no more for a while. Then he looked toward Miss Braithwaite and said, "I guess we're going to have to kill you two. We bumped off one bull already." It was a lie in a further attempt to frighten the unwilling passengers, since the escapees hadn't made contact with any officers after leaving the prison.

As the car approached Neosho, Blair indicated he had to visit a rest room. Woods pulled into a service station.

"The lady stays in the car, so don't try nothin'," Dopson warned.

While Blair was in the men's room, the station attendant attempted to check the car's oil but couldn't locate the gauge.

"I'll find it," Dopson volunteered from the back seat. In order for him to get out, Miss Braithwaite had to step out of the car. As Dopson examined the engine, Blair returned. Noting Dopson and Woods were preoccupied with the car, Blair whispered to his companion to run inside the station. Miss Braithwaite ran toward the building.

The convicts pulled pistols from their pockets to cover Blair and the surprised attendant. Blair pleaded with his captors to take his car and leave them behind.

"Come on, Billie, let's scram," Dopson hollered.

The pair jumped in the car and Woods spun the tires on the graveled driveway of the station, headed the car east on Highway 60.

By midafternoon, they were deep in the Mark Twain National Forest of central Missouri. They spent the night sleeping in the car parked on an abandoned road. Woods and Dopson, both born in St. Louis, were anxious to head home. Woods, who was twenty-two, was actually Harold Wesley Harris, born to William and Pearl Harris, the only son among six children. He had used his own name during his first brush with the law in 1926, when he was picked up in Great Bend, Kansas, for investigation, and later, in February, 1928, when the St. Louis police picked him up for burglary and larceny. But four months later, when he entered the federal penitentiary at Atlanta, at the age of seventeen, on a stolen auto rap, he served under the name of "Billie Kennedy." Arrests in Mobile, Alabama, in May 1930, and East St. Louis, Illinois, a month later were booked under the name of "William Harris."

He was released on a stolen-car charge in East St. Louis and headed west. He worked as a field hand near Macksville, Kansas, got paid, and hitchhiked to Dodge City. He saw a parked Chevrolet coach belonging to M. V. McCormick of Satanta, which he promptly stole. He headed west on Highway 50 to Garden City, where he was spotted by Officer Harold Swartley. The policeman forced the stolen car to the curbing at Second and Laurel streets, but Woods leaped from the car and disappeared between some houses. Swartley started searching and discovered the suspect walking nonchalantly along the street two blocks away. The officer's riot gun convinced the young man he should come to police headquarters. He was returned to Dodge City and jailed. He gave his name as Billie Woods.

He was sent to the Hutchinson reformatory for the theft, but when he attempted to escape, was transferred to the state prison to serve five to fifteen years. When he arrived in Lansing, he was only nineteen years old.

Dopson, who was nineteen at the time of the break, was the youngest of the fugitives. Born on July 30, 1913, he left home at sixteen after completing the eighth grade. His father had died and when his mother married Ollie Dopson, he took his stepfather's name. He went to live with his grandmother in Mississippi for a time, then moved to Springfield, Illinois, when his stepfather and mother moved there. He swiped a car but was released without sentencing and returned to Mississippi with his grandfather on a horse-trading trip. He went back to Springfield for a time, then moved to Oklahoma to work in the wheat fields. He was picked up for vagrancy in Jay, Oklahoma, served a few days in jail before going to Fredonia, Kansas, where he was caught stealing tires. He served seven days in jail and moved on again. He lost track of his family, who had moved to Opelausas, Louisiana, by this time.

On August 4, 1930, he and a friend named Clarence Walker, sometimes called William Clarence Lenay, stole a car in Columbus, Kansas. The two youths drove to Miami, Oklahoma, and had the car, a 1928 Chevrolet coach with disk wheels, about thirty days before being apprehended. Both were returned to Kansas and sent to the reformatory at Hutchinson. Dopson was seventeen. A year later, after an escape attempt, he was sent to Lansing to finish a five to fifteen-year sentence.

Back in Oklahoma, Payton and Conn were not adapting well to the Cooksons. They knew no one, had no money, and had to steal food. As convicted murderers, they feared returning to the Sunflower State until things cooled. Conn had once stolen a car in Batesville, Arkansas, and knew something of the terrain. The pair decided to try their luck in Arkansas.

They drove through the night to Pine Bluff, arriving

early the morning of June 3. Seeking a newer car, Payton pulled alongside one driven by Austin Adams, forcing it to the curb. Adams and his passenger, Beatrice Garner, were taken hostage. Payton headed west on Highway 270, strangely back toward Oklahoma, all the while bragging of their exploits as killers and escapees. The petrified couple listened in abject fear. Near the border, Payton and Conn decided to release their captives. Once again in Oklahoma, the escapees drove through the Cooksons to a small creek outside of Bartlesville, where they camped out. For the next few days, they continued to steal food to exist. They were becoming desperate.

Dopson and Woods felt they needed a better car to continue their journey to St. Louis. Near Fredericktown, Missouri, they spotted McBride Rayfield and Callie Stewart target shooting alongside the road. The coupe was abandoned and Rayfield's larger car commandeered. Four hours later, the escapees and their hostages arrived in St. Louis. Rayfield and Stewart were released unharmed.

Sunday, June 4, 1933, proved to be the most trying day in Frank Sawyer's life. When he left his companions the previous day to strike out on his own with only Clark's fifty cents in his pocket, he couldn't possibly have foreseen such exasperations. He had started out on foot, and had little success hitching rides. It had been blazing hot, and he spent much of the afternoon sitting alongside the road in the shade. That night he slept in a field.

He started thumbing rides again early Sunday morning. At 7:30 a.m., two farmers, Otis Fox and Jerome Lawrence, noticed the overalls-clad hitchhiker and decided to give a "fellow farmer" a lift. Sawyer settled into the back seat of the car and then drew a pistol from his overalls pocket. He took over the wheel, but within miles the car simply quit running. Mr. and Mrs. Fred Gray of Lawton happened by. Sawyer waved them to a halt, took them as hostages, and left Fox and Lawrence with their stalled vehicle.

Seven miles down the road, the Gray machine blew a tire near the hamlet of Middleburg. Again, Sawyer flagged a passing car, this one belonging to Mr. and Mrs. J. H. Strongfield. He piled the Grays in with the Strongfields and continued the journey. Five miles outside of Chickasha, the latest machine developed a steering-rod problem. Sawyer had adequate reason to curse, particularly the products Detroit was putting out.

The Strongfield car limped into the farmyard of Mrs. Mary Hawkins.

"You got a car?" Sawyer demanded of the farm woman.

"Yes."

"Then start it."

Mrs. Hawkins wouldn't budge.

Sawyer stared helplessly at the resolute farm woman, then walked to the barn to locate the car. Once he got the Hawkins car running, he loaded in the Grays and Strongfields and took off along Highway 62. The ancient car wheezed and coughed until Sawyer was convinced he would have to steal yet another one. He chugged into another farmyard a half-dozen miles later. Olin Morris and his son were working in a field near the house when the visitors jerked into the driveway. Sawyer took Morris and his son and the Morris machine, along with the Strongfields, but left the travel-weary Grays. Unbelievably, seven miles north of Gracemont, the car's engine began to miss badly. The wild-eyed Sawyer was so mad, he got out of the car and ordered the hostages to drive on.

"I'll walk," he stated in total desperation.

As the Morrises and Strongfields watched, Sawyer ran into a cornfield and disappeared.

Nearby, Bob Goodfellow, the Caddo County clerk, was

lunching with his sister, Lois, an Oklahoma A & M student. A knock at the door revealed a stranger with a pistol in his hand.

"That your car out front?" the stranger wanted to know. Goodfellow said it was.

"You two go get in it," the man ordered.

Goodfellow took the wheel, his sister and Sawyer climbed in the back seat.

A few miles down the road, Goodfellow decided to run the car into the ditch rather than continue. He suddenly whipped the car hard to the right and into the ditch. Sawyer was livid.

"Okay, wise guy, you two get out and flag down the next car," he instructed. He then moved out of sight behind the wrecked machine.

If Sawyer couldn't believe his ill fortune to this point, he was in for an even bigger surprise. The first car to come along contained Sheriff Horace Crisp and Deputy Al Marlow, who had received a number of complaints about an inordinate number of stolen cars the past few hours. As they approached the wrecked car, the sheriff recognized Goodfellow.

"Hey, Al, that's Bob Goodfellow. Looks like they've had a bad one."

The sheriff halted alongside the Goodfellow car and alighted. Sawyer leaped from behind the ditched machine and grabbed Goodfellow. He fired a shot that sent the sheriff and deputy diving to the ground. Crisp returned a shot that passed through Goodfellow's leg and tore into Sawyer's wrist. Miss Goodfellow, seeing her brother's wound, went berserk. She jumped on Sawyer's back, scratching and clawing like a person possessed. While Crisp held his revolver next to Sawyer's head, Deputy Marlow pulled the screaming girl off the outlaw's back. Crisp picked up Sawyer's gun and whacked him over the head with it, thus ending Sawyer's most atrocious day. He was taken to the Chickasha jail, was picked up by Oklahoma prison officials on Tuesday and returned to McAlester to finish his murder sentence. Kansas would have to wait to get him back.

Early reports following the break pointed to the Cooksons as the most likely destination for the escapees, and when Bechtel was picked up in Oklahoma, lawmen were positive both groups were there. But when Dopson and Woods were reported in Missouri, and Conn and Payton in Arkansas, law forces became divided, and organized deployment was eliminated. With Sawyer's capture, two of the eleven were back in custody, but all of the "big fish" were still loose.

# The Web Is Spun

# 12

The governor of Kansas, Alf Landon, was embarrassed by the escape. He called in his state police director, Wint Smith.

"I want those men back, Wint," the governor stated. "What are you going to do?"

"There's nothing we can do until they come out of Oklahoma," Smith responded, "unless you can get Governor Murray to give us special Oklahoma police credentials. Then we can go after them."

Oklahoma governor "Alfalfa Bill" Murray was having his own problems with Pretty Boy Floyd. "The Robin Hood of the Cooksons" was becoming a myth with the country folks. Stories, which were untrue, of Floyd burning mortgages in banks he robbed were being repeated all over the country. Floyd dashed around the hills like a rabbit. Murray decided to flush him out of the Cooksons, once and for all. He detailed every available officer to get Floyd. This

135

forced Clark, Underhill, Davis, and Brady to remain in the Oklahoma City–Shawnee area as they waited for Bailey to recover. Without Bailey to plot their bank jobs and run the cat roads, they felt the risk was too great. Underhill, incensed when he learned Oklahoma state officers had raided his uncle's farm in Pontotoc County, was becoming increasingly ugly. He wanted to shoot every policeman he encountered. Clark and Brady could hardly control the psychotic killer.

By June 10, Bailey's leg had mended to the point he could walk around his apartment, but not well enough for the stress of a bank job. Clark heard about an easy mark in the town of Black Rock, Arkansas, and decided the boys could wait no longer.

Dopson and Woods found conditions tough in St. Louis. The depression had hit the Mississippi River town hard and jobs were scarce. Woods wanted to move on.

"I'd like to run down to Mexico," he told Dopson. "There's lots of action down there. We might run a little booze back into the States."

Dopson reluctantly agreed and the morning of June 8, they started for Del Rio, Texas, in the same car they'd stolen in Fredericktown. They arrived the next afternoon, spent a rip-roaring night, and decided the morning of June 10 that it was too hot to go on across the border. Woods suggested going to Dallas to try their luck. They headed north on Highway 377.

By midday they neared the little town of Rocksprings. Woods awakened his dozing companion.

"Want an Orange Crush or something?"

"Yeah, let's gas up and get a cold pop."

Dopson took over the wheel when they pulled out of Rocksprings. Woods immediately dropped off to sleep, still feeling the effects of the wild night before.

As the miles droned by, Dopson had trouble keeping his eyes open. Suddenly, he nudged his sleeping companion.

"Wake up, Billie, and tell me if I'm dreamin'."

The drowsy Woods looked up the highway where Dopson was pointing.

"Ain't that a couple of gals up ahead?" Dopson asked.

"Sure as hell is," the now wide-awake Woods replied.

Dopson braked the car to a stop where two young women were standing alongside the road. One was carrying a baby and holding another small child by the hand.

"Can you give us a ride into Junction?" one of the women asked.

"Farther than that if you'd like," Woods smiled, opening the door for them.

They carried on an animated conversation until the car approached the town of Junction. Dopson spotted a road-block in the highway just southwest of the city, but too late to turn off on a side road. He decided to bluff it out, realizing the blockade was probably set up by the customs department to catch liquor runners coming up from Mexico.

Customs agents J. A. Tilley and W. E. Kilborn had indeed set up such a roadblock and were stopping cars randomly for examination. Prohibition of beverages stronger than "three point two" beer was still the law of the land until November and the agents were enforcing the statute. Highway 377 had become a veritable pipeline as smugglers found it the fastest and shortest route from Mexico to parched Dallas. As the car approached, Tilley stepped to the center of the pavement and held up his right hand. Dopson casually drew the car to a halt. Kilborn walked to the driver's side, displayed his badge, and asked the occupants to evacuate in order to search the car for alcohol. Tilley, who had been studying Woods's face, suddenly whipped his service revolver from its holster under his coat.

"Hold it, Killy. This guy's one of those Kansas escapees,"

he shouted to his companion. Kilborn stepped back and drew his gun.

Tilley had studied the wanted posters of the eleven convicts and had no trouble identifying Woods. A close look convinced the agent that Dopson was another of the escapees.

Kilborn ordered the convicts into the federal car, and Tilley and the women and children followed in the car Dopson had been driving. Kilborn's shotgun was lying alongside him in the front seat, but he thought it was not loaded. As they neared Junction, Woods grabbed the gun. Kilborn grabbed the barrel and attempted to wrest it away from the convict. Suddenly a shot ripped through the car door. Kilborn had overlooked a shell in the chamber. The car swerved dangerously from side to side as the driver and the wiry Woods battled for control of the gun. Dopson, next to the door on the passenger side, watched helplessly as the pair struggled. The car careened into a ditch and jarred to a halt. Tilley stopped behind the wrecked government car and covered the escapees with his revolver. The rest of the trip into town was completed with the four men and two women and children in one car.

"I'll never go back to Kansas," Woods screamed as they locked him in the Kimble County jail. Early the next morning, he managed to pick the lock on his cell door, got into the prisoner "run around," an exercise area, but couldn't get out of there, and was slammed back in his cell. On June 12, Guard John Sherman, one of the two guards taken by the other group of escapees as a hostage, arrived, along with Guard Wesley Crew, to escort the pair to Lansing. En route home by motor car, the guards rested at Dallas overnight and put the prisoners in the escape-proof jail there. Woods and Dopson had finally got to Dallas.

In Washington, D. C., the FBI's director, J. Edgar Hoover, was eager to utilize the new Lindbergh kidnap law. Nationally, banks were being robbed at the rate of two a day and Hoover knew he had to take the public's mind off the rampant crimes. His ace public-relations man, Courtney Ryley Cooper, hired away from the Kansas City *Star* to direct the first real government campaign of public relations, was working overtime planting articles in papers around the country. Cooper was seeking a spot to inaugurate a new name he'd invented for the FBI agent— "G-man." United States attorney general Homer S. Cummings was upset and embarrassed by the bank-robbing wave and was pressuring Hoover to return public sentiment to the side of law and order. Congress was barking at Hoover's heels about funding, and one senator even wanted to know how a man who had never made an arrest could direct the nation's crime investigations. Hoover was in a bind.

Early on June 17, 1933, the same morning as the Union Station massacre in Kansas City, Davis, Brady, Clark, and two of Clark's friends, Jess Littrell and Bill Shipley, drove into Black Rock, Arkansas. Littrell had cased the bank months before and reported the safe was an old type without a time lock.

Brady and Clark would hit the bank, Davis drive the getaway car. The others were to tend a boat on the Black River, which bordered the town. The plan was to abandon the getaway car at the bridge, cross the river in the boat, and escape in a second car parked on the opposite bank. The bridge was blocked at one end by a toll gate. The river-crossing by boat would circumvent the potential roadblock, the robbers believed.

When Brady and Clark entered the bank, an old man behind the teller's cage was the only person inside. He immediately became suspicious of the two strangers.

"What are you doing in here?" the old man wanted to

know, as Brady walked behind the counter toward the cage.

"Pop, I came in here to get this money," Brady responded, patting him on the back.

It was then Brady noticed a new safe with a time clock had been installed.

Clark went to the front counter, acting as though he were writing a check. Brady produced a pillow case and began stuffing it with silver and bills from the cage, realizing the safe was not possible to crack. The old man watched helplessly with hands held high above his head.

"Come on, Pop, you can put 'em down now. Let's take a walk," Brady ordered, pointing to the door.

Clark and Brady walked on either side of the old man to where Davis was waiting. Citizens never suspected a robbery was under way as neither bandit displayed a gun.

Forcing the old man to accompany them, the bandits drove to the toll bridge. They released the hostage, ran to the river below, and jumped into the boat. The old man was yelling for help in the meantime, and a couple of farmers with shotguns, who happened across the bridge, began peppering the men in the boat below. Midway across the stream, the five bandits noticed two men standing beside their second car. They turned the boat into the current and floated downstream to a spot they thought was safer. Wading in mud up to their knees, the robbers chose to stash the silver money under a log, returning several days later to retrieve the loot. They hid in the weeds and trees along the riverbank until dark, then walked until they found a farmhouse.

Clark and Brady knocked on the door while the others remained out of sight.

"Howdy, we been fishing down on the river and our car is about fifteen miles upstream," the smooth-talking Brady told the farmer who answered his knock. "Can you drive us into town? We'll make it worth your while."

The farmer explained he was eating his supper, but would be able to drive them into Walnut Ridge shortly. They waited outside until the farmer finished his meal.

At the edge of town, the robbers noticed a lot of activity and realized the law was searching for the Black Rock bandits. They had the farmer drop them off in the outskirts, where he took the ten-dollar bill they handed him and left without a word.

Clark had seen a car enter a nearby garage, and before the driver could get into his house, he was jumped by the robbers. The weary, mud-stained men crawled into the car and roared out of town toward Oklahoma.

They drove until they reached Muskogee, where Clark had lived much of his life. He knew every street in town, had several friends who would hide them until they could get cleaned up. But he sensed something was amiss. He told his companions to drive on to Oklahoma City. The next day, they learned there had been a robbery in Muskogee and a merchant killed, which resulted in a giant searching operation by the police department. They also learned five men had been killed the previous day at the Union Station in Kansas City.

Harvey Bailey picked up the *Daily Oklahoman* and was shocked to discover he was a prime suspect in the Union Station killings. Still confined because of his wounded knee, he had to wait until later, when the doctor arrived, to vent his ire.

"Doc, read here what it says about me," he bellowed before the doctor could even get his hat off.

"Yes, I read about it earlier. Don't worry. I'll sign an affidavit you were under my care at the time."

"They accused me of the Denver mint job, the Lincoln heist, and everything else that's happened in the last ten years," Bailey fumed.

When the nurse, now on duty only part time, arrived to

care for his daily needs, his tirade started all over again. "I'm a thief, not a killer," he announced.

"Harvey," the doctor interrupted, "I'd say you are getting better."

The next day, Clark and Brady visited Bailey.

"Now the damned FBI is saying we wuz in on that Kansas City shooting," Brady said. "We ought to let 'em know we wuz in Arkansas."

"A good idea," Clark agreed. "What do you think, Harve?"

"Yeah, but how?"

"Why don't we send 'em a letter and put our fingerprints on it," Brady suggested. Oddly enough, Pretty Boy Floyd, also being accused of the massacre (along with every other known criminal on the loose) may have had the same idea. He supposedly mailed a postcard to the Kansas City Police Department from Springfield, Missouri, on June 21 in which he proclaimed innocence of the crime. Handwriting specialists believed it was not Floyd's writing on the card and reasoned he'd had a friend send it. Actually, he was hiding in Iowa. But the letter from Clark, Davis, Brady, Underhill, and Bailey was legitimate and bore their fingerprints stamped in motor oil. The FBI dismissed the letter and continued to claim the Bailey-Underhill gang was responsible for the massacre.

Bailey, hampered by his injury, wasn't the only one biding his time. Conn and Payton continued to live like animals, camping along secluded creek beds, foraging for food, and existing off the proceeds of an occasional robbery. Payton was waiting for the right conditions to return to more familiar territory in Labette County, Kansas, where he still had friends. Although born in Adair, Oklahoma, on July 16, 1909, Payton spent much of his youth in the Kansas county. After serving some time in the state reformatory at Granite for stealing chickens at the age of eighteen, Payton and three other out-of-work youths robbed the Edna, Kansas, bank of $2,000 on October 15, 1930. They fled to Texas and were caught near Stinnett with $1,200 of the loot. Park Magness and John Nichols made a guilty plea and were imprisoned, but Payton and George Magness pleaded innocent. It was several weeks before they stood trial, time enough for escape plans to be made. Following their conviction on the bank-robbing charges, they were taken to the jail in Oswego, the county seat. Sheriff Al Coad, Deputy Melvin Hamilton, and a special deputy, Roy McLean, prepared to drive the prisoners to Lansing. As they were led to the sheriff's car, manacled and shackled, Magness's wife ran up to him and pinned a flower on his shirt with a steel pin. When she gave her husband a final hug, she slipped a small-caliber pistol in his pocket.

Sheriff Coad decided to drive to Girard to pick up Highway 73E north to the prison. At the outskirts of Girard, the prisoners demanded to use a rest room. Coad spotted a roadside privy and allowed the prisoners to use it, keeping the door open. Magness managed to slip the pin from the flower and, using his body as a shield, quickly picked the lock on his handcuffs. They hobbled back to the car and the officers didn't notice his cuffs were open. As the journey resumed, Coad continued to drive. McLean, in the back seat with the two prisoners, was sitting behind him. Hamilton, next to Coad in the front seat, pulled a sack of peppermint candy from his pocket. He turned to offer the prisoners some of the candy just as Magness pulled the pistol from his pocket.

Magness pulled the trigger and the bullet tore into Hamilton's face between the eyes. At the same instant, Payton jammed his shoulder into McLean, pinning the deputy against the car door so that he couldn't draw his gun. Again Magness pulled the trigger, the bullet striking the slumped Hamilton in the head. Magness then pointed his gun toward Coad, who was attempting to steer the car while reaching for his gun. The pistol in Magness's hand roared again and Coad, a bullet in his neck, let loose of the wheel. The wildly careening car skidded across the highway. Coad, blood streaming from his face where the bullet had exited, managed to free his gun and, without looking backward, pointed the barrel to the rear. Magness fired another shot, the bullet ripping the brim of Coad's hat. Then, Coad pulled the trigger of his .45. The shot, fired blindly, struck Magness in the head, killing him instantly. Coad lost consciousness and the car plunged into a ditch, struck a culvert, and overturned. Miraculously, Coad crawled out of the wreckage and held his pistol on Payton until McLean could free himself. Passing motorists took Coad to the Fort Scott hospital while McLean accompanied Payton to the jail. For his part in the murder Payton was sentenced for twenty years to life.

Deputy Hamilton's wife was a patient in a Kansas City hospital when she heard of her husband's death. Their oldest son, Earl, was a big-league pitcher and not at home at the time. Two young children had to claim their father's body.

Conn was also a convicted murderer. His mother died when he was an infant, and when his father died in 1923, while Kenneth was in the fifth grade, he took to the road. The only relative was a married sister living in Texas and he didn't wish to live with her. He stole cars and bummed around the country to exist. In 1930, when he was seventeen, he was sent to the Boys Industrial Home in Golden, Colorado, for car theft, but escaped. He and another seventeen-year-old, Ernest Shaw, were hitchhiking their way east when picked up in the little Kansas town of Jetmore on a vagrancy investigation. They jumped the single officer, took his gun and car, and fled. At Pratt, they held up a man named George Atchison. Conn, not familiar with the .38 automatic they'd taken from the Jetmore policeman, accidentally pulled the trigger and Atchison was struck by the bullet just above the navel. He died instantly. The killers fled to Oklahoma where they tried to steal another car in Pottawatomie County. Officers apprehended the pair and, in February, 1931, turned them over to the state of Kansas. Conn arrived in Lansing to serve a life sentence on May 20, 1931.

Since both were escaped murderers, Conn and Payton felt Kansas was not a safe place to return to.

Bailey summoned his cohorts on July 1 to inform them he was ready.

"Boys, we need a chopper. You rob a bank with a pistol and somebody might get brave and you'll have to shoot him. Go in with a machine gun and nobody ever gets brave," he philosophized. "Any ideas?"

"To hell with a chopper. Let's get some money," Underhill yelled.

The others agreed that, since a machine gun was not readily available, they get on with the task at hand.

"There's a bank over in Clinton that looks pretty good," Bailey said. "Let's run over and case it. But I don't like it without a tommy gun."

On July 2, Bailey, Brady, and Clark drove to the Custer County town, looked over the First National Bank, and decided it was easy enough to hit the following day. That night, the others agreed they had to dump Underhill. He was more irrational than ever.

"We'll let him in on this job, then get rid of him," Bailey determined.

On July 3, they piled into a new Ford V-8 Bailey had bought and drove to Clinton. The thermometer showed 103 degrees when Bailey, aided by his cane, strode through the bank door at precisely 2:55 p.m.

"Everybody freeze. This is a stick-up," the routine words were barked. Within two minutes, the clerks and customers were herded to the back of the bank where passersby couldn't see them. Brady piled the cash into his "tote bag," the familiar pillowcase, while the rest trained guns on the captives. Georgia Loving and Thelma Selle, bank customers, were ordered outside as hostages. Davis, guarding the door, told the women to go to the car. Just then Clark arrived at the door with the bank vice president, George Zahn.

"Got no room for him," Davis announced, and the relieved bank official retreated as the bandits fled out the door.

Bailey, Clark, and Miss Loving got in the back seat, and Miss Selle was told to ride the running board. As the car sped away, Underhill tossed roofing nails into the street. The women were released a few blocks away since there was no pursuit.

Running the cat roads until dark, the bandits drove south to the Salt Fork of the Red River, where they counted their loot in the car's headlights. It came to $11,000. The group then drove back north to a wooded area near Shawnee, where they spent the night with a friend of Underhill's.

Conn was anxious to get back to civilized living. It was July and he was getting antsy.

"Sonny, we better do something quick before I go crazy," he warned his companion. "Let's go rob a bank and get out of this country."

Payton felt things had cooled sufficiently for them to try their luck. But his knowledge of available banks was confined to Labette County in Kansas. The boys switched their camping headquarters to Caney Creek. Although unaware of it, they had been spotted almost as soon as they arrived. Local law officers, not knowing it was Conn and Payton, watched the campers for anything suspicious. After several trips to the town of Altamont, Payton felt the Labette

County State Bank was ripe. It was July 14 when Conn and Payton made their move.

Cashier Isaac McCarty and his wife, Colene, assistant cashier, were busy preparing the bank for the 9 a.m. opening when they spotted the strangers cruising down Altamont's main street. Driving a car stolen weeks before from J. W. Chinn in Bartlesville, the pair surveyed the bank carefully, deciding to park on a side street west of the bank's door. McCarty, well aware of the number of small-town bank heists, watched closely as the strangers parked their car, then strode briskly toward the front door, which was still locked. The men had miscalculated the time. They stood uncomfortably by the door. McCarty decided he'd go "upstairs."

"Upstairs," above the bank vault and reached by a stepladder, was a cubicle that had been constructed in the event of a suspected bank robbery. A rifle, shotgun, and ammunition were stored in the tiny room. A small, curtained window permitted an overall view of the lobby.

Colene walked around the counter and unlocked the door. The two men entered.

"We're a little early, I guess," Payton smiled at her. "But we want to make a deposit."

"That's all right," Mrs. McCarty replied, walking back behind the counter.

As she reached her station, she noticed Conn had pulled a gun.

"Put 'em up," he snarled.

"I've already got 'em up," the amazingly cool young woman responded.

Payton then walked to the bank's small conference room where W. H. Drumheller, the president, was discussing a business deal with A. H. McCarty, the vice president (and Isaac's father), and A. O. Sachs, a rural mail carrier and bank customer.

"Stick 'em up," Payton ordered.

The elder McCarty, who was writing, didn't bother to look up.

"Stick 'em up or I'll kill you," Payton screamed.

McCarty looked up, saw the gun, and wasted no time getting his hands aloft. Payton then marched the three men behind the teller's cage and instructed them to begin sacking money. Isaac McCarty, watching from above, had already pressed the burglar alarm, and Altamont citizens were filling the street to see what was happening. He was waiting for the bandits to place the victims inside the vault, a common procedure, before he opened fire.

The nervous Conn, holding his gun on Mrs. McCarty, noticed the crowd gathering outside the bank, some armed with rifles.

"My God, Sonny, there's people out there."

Payton ran to the door.

"Grab that gal and let's get outta here," he told Conn.

"Come on," Conn told Colene, "you're coming with us."

Still calm, the unruffled cashier said: "I'm ready to go."

As Payton stood by the door, young McCarty saw his chance. He fired the shotgun. Pellets tore into Payton's face and shoulders. He fell to the floor, his face a bloody pulp. Conn, not knowing the source of the blast, ran to the door. Again McCarty cut loose and Conn took a load in the left shoulder, but didn't fall. Outside, Robert Schooley, manager of the Kansas Home Telephone Company, stood in the doorway of the Baker Bros. Garage, diagonally across from the bank, and shot out the tires in the bandits' car. Conn, thinking the shot that ripped into his shoulder had come from outside, grabbed Colene, pulling her down behind the counter. He was trapped and didn't know which way to turn. Clutching an automatic pistol in his right hand, holding Colene's arm with the other, he shouted at the elder McCarty.

"I'll kill the girl and some of the rest of you. Have that shooting stopped," the panic-stricken bandit screamed.

"I can't, unless I go outside," the banker answered.

"Then go out there and tell them, and come right back in," Conn yelled.

As the elder McCarty started toward the door, Ike, now with the rifle, let go a third shot. The bullet struck Conn in the back and tore into his lungs. He let out a half-shriek, half-moan and mumbled, "Oh, my God," as he fell against the counter.

Colene, not realizing Ike knew her position, yelled at him not to shoot.

"I'm over here," she screamed.

Ike could see her clearly and didn't hesitate to fire once more into Conn's back. The high-powered bullet passed through his body and splintered the floor behind the coun ter. Conn toppled sideways along the counter, dead when he hit the floor.

Colene, who had been so calm throughout the episode, jumped up and ran out the door. She didn't quit running until inside Gearhiser's Cafe, a half-block away.

Two men left the crowd in front of the bank and entered the building.

"Everything clear?" one asked Ike as he was climbing down the ladder from the cubicle.

"Yeah, they're both dead," the young teller answered.

Just then, Payton half-rose from the floor.

"Get me to a hospital. I've got fifteen hundred dollars," he pleaded, apparently believing money would get him faster medical treatment.

Dr. R. F. Roller, the town physician, was called to aid the bloody Payton. Both eyes were shot out and his face, neck, and shoulders pitted with buckshot.

"What's your name and where are you from?" the doctor asked.

"I have no name and I'm from nowhere," the bandit replied.

"What's your partner's name?"

"Is he dead?" Payton asked in return.

"Yes, he's dead and you're going to die."

"Well, I'm Alva Payton and my partner is Kenneth Conn. We broke outta the pen at Lansing, Memorial Day." As Payton was being carried to a car to be driven to the Oswego hospital, Sheriff Bill Bitner arrived. He recognized both bandits, remembering Payton from his days as a youth in Labette County. Conn's body was removed to the Martin and Fritz Funeral Home in Altamont, where it remained unclaimed. The state finally paid for the burial in the Altamont cemetery, off to one side from the decent folks, the grave unmarked except for a tiny metal plate in which the name and date of burial were scratched by hand.

Although blinded and scarred, Payton quickly recovered and was soon back at Lansing. An examination of the stolen car revealed two high-powered rifles, ammunition, extra license plates, and a week's supply of food, including a cake.

In Oklahoma City, Clark, Davis, and Bailey laid plans to add another bank to their list. Brady and his wife, Leona, were spending the loot from the Clinton job with her relatives in Des Moines. Underhill had returned to the Cooksons where he was visiting with some old friends, including Charley Cotner, Enos Smiddy, and a divorcee named Hazel Jarrett Hudson. She was a sister of the infamous Jarrett brothers.

Bailey selected the Kingfisher, Oklahoma, bank as the next target.

"But I ain't doing no more jobs without a machine gun," he warned Clark and Davis. "I'm going down to Paradise and see if Kelly has a gun he'll let us use. He owes me a favor."

He was referring to the $1,000 Machine Gun Kelly had borrowed in Kansas City. Paradise was a small Texas town where Robert G. "Boss" Shannon, the stepfather of Kelly's wife, operated a farm used as a criminal hideout.

Bailey drove his new Ford to Paradise, accompanied by Clark. Kelly wasn't there, but Shannon let them borrow Kelly's tommy gun, which they promised to return in a few days. As it turned out, Kelly and Albert Bates, another bank robber of note, were laying plans to kidnap an Oklahoma City oilman, Charles Urschel, and were running the cat roads between Paradise and Oklahoma City. Had Bailey known, Kelly could have delivered the gun to Oklahoma City.

On July 22, Kelly and Bates walked onto the verandah of the Urschel home in Oklahoma City, kidnapped the oilman as he and his wife were playing bridge with another couple. He was blindfolded, driven to the Shannon farm, and held for $200,000 ransom. Nine days later he was released unharmed when the ransom was paid in Kansas City. One of the great criminal investigations in American history followed.

Urschel, although blindfolded, meticulously made mental notes of seemingly insignificant sounds that led to a raid on the farm. He remembered the rattling of wooden boards while the kidnappers' car crossed a long bridge (which turned out to be one crossing the Canadian River southeast of Oklahoma City), an airplane that passed overhead daily, and sounds of a mule braying and a squeaky well pulley. He managed to see a few items when the blindfold was removed to permit him to write the ransom notes. The airplane flights became the key as it was determined the craft was running the mail route between Fort Worth and Amarillo, based on the times Urschel heard it overhead. By casually asking his guard what time it was when he heard the plane's engine, he ascertained the schedule. Agents were led to the Paradise area as the spot the plane would have been above at specific times that Urschel noted.

After obtaining Kelly's tommy gun, Bailey and Clark returned to Oklahoma City. Underhill had come back from the Cooksons and wanted to rejoin the gang. Bailey acquiesced because the Kingfisher job required a fourth man. Since Brady was visiting in Iowa, Underhill was assigned the task of manning a second getaway car, where he would be less likely to shoot someone.

Clark, Davis, and Bailey drove to the People's National Bank in Kingfisher on August 9 and promptly at 1:45 p.m. entered the front door. They herded the customers and bank clerks to the rear, goaded by Bailey's machine gun. As Clark and Davis filled their tote bags with cash, a large man wearing the uniform of a Coca-Cola delivery truck driver asked Clark if he could get a drink from a ten-gallon keg of iced water on the counter.

"You can drink as much as you want to, brother," Clark told the man, continuing to fill his sack with paper money.

After filling the bags, Clark and Davis backed toward the door, grabbing the Coke man and two others as hostages. As no chase resulted, the hostages were left at the edge of town, unharmed.

When the fleeing bandits reached the Cimarron River, where Underhill was waiting with the second car on the far bank, the bank robbers attempted to ford the shallow but tricky stream. The car became mired so they waded to the opposite shore. Underhill drove them to Shawnee, where they split the loot. At Kingfisher, bank officials quickly picked out Bailey, Clark, and Davis from the photos of the Kansas escapees.

Bailey and Clark continued to the safety of Pike's cabin to spend the night. Bailey stayed on while he dyed his hair brown, but Clark decided to drive to Tulsa for a time. They agreed to meet two days later at high noon on a road near Shawnee to make future plans. Clark contacted Brady, who joined in the meeting, on August 11, to discuss a bank up in Brainerd, Minnesota, that Bailey had in mind. Bailey, at the conclusion of the meeting, headed for Paradise to return Kelly's machine gun to him. Bailey had left the bulk of his cash from the Kingfisher job in Pike's care, taking only $100 and a bag of silver coins Pike didn't want around the cabin. He drove through the day and night, arriving about 3 a.m. at the Shannon farm. Shannon awakened when Bailey's headlights flashed into the yard.

Bailey placed the machine gun on the porch.

"Hi, Boss," he greeted the old man. "Is George around?"

"Naw, him and Kathryn took off last week. But he left an envelope here for you." He returned with a sealed envelope, which Bailey tore open. He counted out $1,000 in small bills. There was no note, but Bailey knew it was repayment of the loan he'd made Kelly a year before. None of them knew that the bills, part of the Urschel ransom, had been marked. Bailey jammed the money in his pocket.

Ora Shannon came to the porch and asked Bailey if he needed a meal. Bailey, unable to find restaurants open along the way, was hungry. As the old woman cooked, Bailey and Boss chatted a while.

Then Boss called Kelly and Kathryn in Chicago, where they were hiding while waiting for things to cool from the Urschel kidnapping. Bailey got on and talked to Kelly about the return of the machine gun.

"Harve, you'd better clear out of there," Kelly warned. "Things are pretty hot right now."

"I know," Bailey responded. "I'll catch a little shut-eye and get moving."

"Here, Kathryn wants to say hello," Kelly said, turning the instrument over to his wife.

"Hey, Old Man, you'd better get outta there," she warned, echoing her husband's words. "Cops is everywhere these days."

Bailey said again he would be leaving in the morning and hung up.

After eating, Bailey handed Ora a sack full of coins from the Kingfisher job as payment for her hospitality.

"You look tired, Harve. Why don't you catch a few winks?" Shannon suggested. Because of the heat, Bailey spread out on a cot in the yard, placing a Winchester rifle on the ground beside him and a .45 pistol under his pillow. He instantly fell sound asleep.

The extensive notes that Urschel had kept were paying off. In Dallas, the FBI's crack agent Gus Jones was assembling data that pointed to the Paradise area. In nine days of captivity, Urschel had compiled some seventy-five observations that Jones put together. They were looking for a three-room farm house in run-down condition somewhere south of Oklahoma City, about fourteen driving hours away where it had rained hard one day followed by a steady day-long drizzle, and on a direct airline route between Amarillo and Fort Worth. What seemed like a needle in a haystack wasn't actually that elusive, since calculations of the airline flight showed the plane would be passing over the general Wise County area at the times Urschel noted. Many mysterious big cars had been seen in the Shannon farm area, so it was the first place in the county officers began checking. Son Armon Shannon lived in a three-room shack not far from his father's place. Investigators began there. An "agent" for a farm-loan company called on Armon, pointing out the need for a loan as he casually glanced around the grounds seeking the mule Urschel had heard braying. Inside the house, the investigator sought a high-chair Urschel had spotted when his blindfold was removed to write a ransom letter. A visit to the well for a fresh drink revealed the water was highly mineralized, something Urschel had also noted.

On the morning of August 12, agents surrounded the farm. Gus Jones moved stealthily toward the house and was surprised to see a man sleeping on a cot in the yard. "Doc" White and "Two-Gun Billy" Winstead, both FBI agents, were alongside Jones when he touched the muzzle of a machine gun under the sleeping man's nose. "My

God," thought Jones, "it's Harvey Bailey."

Jones stepped back as the sleeping man opened his eyes.

"All right, Harvey. It's all up."

Bailey slowly rose to a sitting position.

"By God, a man's got to sleep sometime, hasn't he?" was Bailey's only comment. He made no move toward his guns. Agents quickly tied his hands.

"I know when I'm beat and I was beat bad this time, wasn't I?" Bailey told the officers as he was led away. Other agents entered the house and routed Boss and Ora Shannon, the only ones in the house at the time. In the kitchen, officers found the bag of silver Bailey had given Mrs. Shannon. The $1,000 in the envelope Kelly had left plus another $100 were found on Bailey. On the raid with the FBI officers were four Fort Worth detectives, J. W. Swinney, Ed Weatherford, C. C. Carmichael, and Herman Shiflett. The kidnap victim, Charles Urschel, armed with a shotgun, also accompanied the raiding party, easily identifying everyone involved except Bailey. The other members of the party of fifteen raiders included Dallas police officers and Oklahoma City lawmen Bill Eads and Clarence Hurt, who came with Urschel. Dallas Department of Justice chief R. H. Colvin was also present.

After securing the Shannons and Bailey, the party moved to Armon Shannon's shack and arrested him and his wife, Oleta. Another Shannon son, oddly named Other, was brought from his neighboring farm to care for his twelve-year-old sister and Pauline Fry, a step-sister who lived with the elder Shannon and his second wife. The accused, including Bailey, were rushed to the same Dallas jail that had held Woods and Dopson exactly two months earlier. Bailey and the others were charged with kidnapping. Bailey was taken to the ninth floor, and his entry read: "One Jones, hold for investigation." The jailers didn't know the identity of their prisoner until morning, so secretive were the federal officers.

When asked by the press about Bailey's capture, Agent Jones said the arrest cleared up "the Union Station massacre and the Urschel kidnapping." What about Pretty Boy Floyd, one of the reporters asked.

"He had nothing at all to do with the Union Station job," was the reply. "Nor the Urschel kidnapping."

Strangely enough, Bates had been arrested in Denver about the same time. Agents had gone to his home, probably on a tip from his wife, and surprised him there. He surrendered without a fight and was rushed to Oklahoma City to stand trial with the others.

In Kansas, prison officials were breathing easier. Of the Memorial Day escapees, Conn was dead; Bechtel, Sawyer, Woods, Dopson, Payton, and Bailey were behind bars. Only Clark, Davis, Brady, and Underhill remained free.

## The Hoover Era Begins

# 13

Bailey's capture, however inadvertent, proved a bonanza for the hard-pressed Department of Justice. Hoover was quick to capitalize on the situation, amplifying the deeds of the dangerous criminals his FBI agents had snared. When Bailey's bond was set at an amazing $100,000, headlines across the nation trumpeted the information. Although the Shannons were unquestionably tied to the Urschel kidnapping and there was considerable doubt about Bailey's participation, the government recognized he was the one to go after. There was little prestige in apprehending lesser criminals such as the Shannon family, who were obviously only guards of the victim. Washington watched carefully as the nation's newspapers pre-tried Bailey for the kidnapping, the Union Station massacre, and various and sundry other major acts. Attorney General Cummings realized Bailey might well be the tool needed for his justice department to regain some of the public's favor and placate Con-

157

gress as well. But J. Edgar Hoover wasn't about to let his FBI become overshadowed in its role in the case, even if it meant sparring with his own boss over the headlines.

When Cummings showed undue interest in the Bailey situation, Hoover informed the press his staff was going to "put Bailey away for life." He failed to mention that the most expeditious manner of doing that would be to turn Bailey over to Kansas authorities to be tried for kidnapping the warden and to complete his bank-robbing sentence. But that wouldn't produce the publicity of a federal trial, and Kansas would get whatever attention resulted.

As the Shannons were small fry, Bates not considered a big leaguer, and Kelly hadn't been caught yet, Bailey represented a bird in the hand to Hoover. Bates was in custody in Denver within hours after Bailey was nailed in Paradise, but the newspapers failed to make much mention of it. Bailey was the premier criminal of the day; he therefore earned public attention, the media felt. Hoover's problem was getting his boss to butt out of the picture.

But Cummings was keenly aware of the publicity potential and put his top assistant, Joseph B. Keenan, on the case. Hoover countered by sending his first assistant, Harold Nathan, to visit Bailey in the Dallas jail in the hope of extracting information to be used against other major criminals such as the Barker gang, the Kellys, of course, and even Pretty Boy Floyd.

Even before Bailey was formally arraigned, the case had taken on a circus aura.

Keenan launched the headline-grabbing campaign with a statement that Bailey should be placed in an iron cage during the trial, with around-the-clock guards with guns at the ready and instructions to shoot if he made any attempt to escape. When the statement hit the newspapers, Keenan's concept of security procedure proved embarrassing to the court. Keenan quickly reduced his proposal to simply having the guards on duty with drawn guns at all times.

Hoover grasped the opportunity to announce he was specifically seeking a long-term prison sentence for Bailey. This forced Keenan to announce: "The government wants every one of these hardened criminals either hanged or electrocuted." Once again, a torrent of public disfavor descended on Keenan.

There seemed little question the general citizenry felt that Bailey, despite his other crimes, was not guilty in the Urschel case, and that the FBI was guessing about his connection in the massacre.

Just when Hoover and Cummings were squaring off for a real battle, Boss Shannon almost blew the whole show. He admitted that Kelly and Bates were the kidnappers, and that he and his family had guarded the victim. But, he added, Bailey had nothing to do with it. The prosecution ignored the confession and sailed ahead with plans to nail Bailey on the Urschel case.

Bailey, in the meanwhile, was concerned over his visit with Nathan, the FBI aide.

"Harvey, right or wrong, we have orders from Washington to put you away. If you tell us a few things we want to know, we could make things a lot easier for you."

Bailey never responded, his brown eyes glaring at the government man.

Bailey was finally arraigned in Fort Worth on the kidnapping charge, then returned to the Dallas jail. The impregnable fortress had been escape-proof in its long history. The first inmate to test it was Houston Wagoner, a murderer, in 1918. He got as far as the first floor before being gunned down. Later, Raymond Hamilton, the partner of Clyde Barrow and Bonnie Parker, decided his 263-year sentence was too long and managed to saw through two bars before being caught. Three other minor attempts were also aborted over the years. Bailey couldn't see much hope of getting out.

On the morning of September 3, Bailey was let out of his

cell for his daily exercise period. When he returned to his bunk, Deputy Jailer Tom Manion sidled to the cell door.

"Find anything under your pillow?" the jailer whispered.

Bailey felt under the pillow. A hacksaw blade and pistol had been placed there. He slowly arose and walked to the cell door where he began a casual conversation with the jailer, never referring to the gun and blade. Manion, as he talked, eventually revealed he was hopeful of some day running for sheriff. Bailey soon realized why the blade and gun had been placed at his disposal. Manion could wait for the break, capture or shoot Bailey, and gain considerable notoriety, the bank robber assessed.

"You know, a man could never get out of this place, but if he did the smart way to go would be right out the front door, 'cause no one would be looking for you to go that way," Bailey mused. The seed was planted in the jailer's mind, Bailey felt. If he made a break, it'd not be out the front door, he thought.

As Bailey's cell was in the isolation block, he could use the saw blade all night without being discovered.

By dawn of the morning of September 4, which was Labor Day, with some of the jail staff given the day off, Bailey had sawed through the two bars necessary for him to slide through the cell door. He tossed a towel over the hole created by the missing bars, drawing no attention since most prisoners hung damp towels to dry in that manner. Bailey's plan was to jump the trusty and guard who brought in breakfast as they stepped off the elevator, then take the elevator to the third floor where the turnkey held the keys to doors and cells. From there he planned to take the elevator to the lobby, jump the guard on duty, and escape through the back door.

Deputy Charles Young and a trusty arrived with the morning meal shortly after 6 a.m. Bailey pointed the pistol, an old Bisley-model Colt .45, at the surprised men, ordered them into a cell where he slammed the door shut. When the elevator returned, Bailey was ready and as soon as the door opened, put the pistol in the operator's face. The inmate never hesitated when Bailey ordered him to the third floor.

Bailey took the turnkey by surprise, placed him in a padded cell for safekeeping, and grabbed a number of keys in the event the back door of the jail was locked. He then instructed the elevator operator to take him to the main floor. Guard Nick Tresp was reading the morning paper and didn't notice as Bailey strode from the elevator. Placing the Bisley next to the guard's ear, Bailey said: "Get up, mister. We're taking a walk."

Tresp arose slowly, instantly recognizing his assailant. "Look, Mr. Bailey, I'll do what you say, just don't shoot."

Moments before, a grocery salesman had gone out the front door of the jail after calling on the commissary. He stopped in the foyer to make notes and happened to glance back into the jail lobby. He saw what was happening and rushed across the street to the office of Sheriff Smoot Schmid. On duty was Officer Gentry Dugat. A deputy, Bud Walker, had just driven up, ready to go to work. The wild-eyed salesman told them what he had seen. The officers rushed to the window but couldn't see inside the jail. Walker ran to his patrol car and Dugat sounded the alarm.

Bailey shoved the guard toward the back door.

"Is that locked?"

"No, sir."

"You gotta car?" Bailey asked.

"Yes, sir. But it's parked across the alley in that filling station lot."

"Let's go. Out the back," Bailey yelled, remembering Manion might be waiting in front.

The pair exited into the alley and Tresp indicated a green Model-A Ford coupe was his. Bailey slid behind the steering wheel.

"Get in," he told Tresp. "I got a hundred thirty-five miles to go and I'm taking you along." Knowing Bailey's reputation, the guard quickly entered the car.

Bailey swung out of the alley just as Deputy Walker arrived in the patrol car. Bailey roared onto Houston Street and headed north. As he passed the jail's front entrance, he noticed two men in a parked car. One was Manion! Bailey chuckled to himself.

Bailey picked up Highway 114 out of Dallas, drove to Grapevine and then to Rhome, curiously skirting within a dozen miles of the Shannon farm at Paradise.

Although the direct route to the Cookson Hills was through Sherman, Bailey took Highway 81 at Rhome, doubled back east on a state road to bypass Denton, and then picked up Highway 77 north to Gainesville. He figured a new bridge at Sherman would be guarded, so he chose to cross the river via the older bridge north of Gainesville. The hunch paid off.

Several days before Labor Day, torrential rains had made a quagmire of the farm-to-market roads. This caused Bailey not to employ the usual cat roads, and he was forced to take Highway 77. Near Marietta, Oklahoma, he found a gravel road that was passable into Ardmore, entering through the Negro section of town.

Once inside Oklahoma, he breathed a bit easier.

"We're okay now," he informed the quaking Tresp.

The Model A was running low on gas when they hit Ardmore. Bailey pulled into a one-pump station at the junction of 77 and 70. A woman came out to serve. Bailey was irritated when she began pumping the handle so the glass bowl indicated gasoline was precisely on the line.

"Ma'am, I'm in a big hurry. Don't bother with that," Bailey told the woman. She inserted the nozzle in the Ford's tank.

A short time before Bailey hit Ardmore, the city's police chief, Hale Dunn, had received a call from Love County sheriff Sam Randolph that Bailey might be heading in that direction. Dunn and two city detectives spotted the green Ford being gassed. The ever-alert Bailey saw them approaching. He leaped in the car, slammed it in low gear, and accelerated. The gasoline hose flew high into the air, spewing gasoline as the stunned woman attendant stood with mouth agape. Bailey headed into the city, hoping to elude the officers on the side streets. The mad chase began, winding through the residential area where many people were just arising on the holiday. The chase ended when Bailey rounded a corner too rapidly, banged into a street curb, crumpling the right front wheel. Tresp leaped from the disabled machine and, with hands held high, yelled: "I'm a jailer! I'm a jailer!"

Chief Dunn walked to Bailey's side of the car.

"I *thought* you couldn't get out of that Dallas jail," the chief said derisively.

"Well, I guess I *got out* all right," Bailey responded.

Bailey was led to the courthouse where a large crowd gathered to see the famed outlaw. When asked how he obtained the gun and hacksaw blade, he said he found them in his mattress, which brought peals of laughter from the press and lawmen. Since it was the truth, Bailey only smiled.

Although the Dallas jail was not federally operated, Bailey was a federal prisoner, so J. Edgar Hoover demanded a complete investigation of the escape. It was a simple matter to tie Manion, one of the few persons who had contact with Bailey prior to the break, with the escape. He and a friend, Grover Bevill, a butcher, were charged with aiding the escape. They claimed the bank robber had offered to share his next bank job with them if they'd help him escape.

Hoover, again embarrassed indirectly by Bailey, ordered the alleged kidnapper and Union Station killer taken to Oklahoma City rather than returned to Dallas. The Shannons had already been transferred to Oklahoma to stand trial. For a time, plans were to transfer Bailey to Kansas City for the massacre trial, but since the Shannons were ready for the kidnapping case, it was determined to send him to Oklahoma City. Shortly thereafter, a federal grand jury laid down a blanket indictment against fourteen persons, including six money-washers in Minneapolis to whom Bates had gone to launder the ransom money.

In mid-August, only the Kellys remained at large of the fourteen indicted, and agents were hot on their trail. When the pair traded in their new Buick on a Cadillac in Cleveland, the FBI picked up the scent. The Kellys fled to Chicago, where they read of the arrest of Bailey and the Shannons. At the same time, they noted that Bates had been picked up in Denver.

Desperate, the Kellys then dumped their Cadillac for a less-conspicuous Chevrolet and headed south. At Davenport, Iowa, they began looking for license plates to steal, finally locating a pair in Des Moines. They hid for a time with Kathryn's relatives near Coleman, Texas, where Kelly buried a machine gun and nearly $1,200 of the ransom money wrapped in an oil slicker. The rest of the money was in Minneapolis. The Kellys continued their flight, moving on to Biloxi, Mississippi, then back to Texas, and once again to Chicago, spending no more than one night anywhere. On September 21, they headed for Kelly's old home town, Memphis, Tennessee.

Kelly had a friend go to Coleman to dig up the money, but the confederate failed to locate it. He sent Kelly a wire at a Memphis apartment. The FBI easily traced the wire and descended on the apartment. It was then the nickname devised by the public-relations department, "G-Man," was put to use.

The agents broke in and Kelly reportedly cowered in the corner shouting: "Don't shoot, G-men, don't shoot." Until he died in 1956, Kelly maintained he never uttered those words, but reporters covering the capture made "G-man" a household word when they sent out their stories using it for the first time.

Kelly's arrest was on September 26, three days after Bailey's trial had begun in Oklahoma City.

The trial was a travesty. The newspapers vigorously pursued every angle, and flashbulbs popped continuously. The most-wanted outlaw in America had been captured and was being showcased. Prior to trial, for the first time in modern American penal history, a man was to be manacled and chained; stripped of all clothing but his B.V.D.s; denied writing material, exercise, and a chair upon which to sit; and surrounded, night and day, by seven machine-gun carrying guards.

Bates joined the Shannons in admitting Bailey had nothing to do with the Urschel case, but the government demanded Bailey stand trial.

The bizarre conditions surrounding the trial gained international attention—just what the government forces desired. Bailey, one of the most-publicized criminals of the era, became the star. As the prosecution squared away to solve two of the century's most notorious crimes, the Union Station massacre and the Urschel kidnapping, Bailey realized he was "it" in a game of jurisprudential tag.

A feverish public greeted the first day of the trial. Hundreds of spectators rushed into the courtroom when the doors were opened. More than one hundred fifty women jammed into the limited seating area, tearing clothing and pushing madly in a quest for a seat. More than a hundred others stood in the corridor outside Judge Edgar S. Vaught's courtroom.

A hush fell over the packed courtroom as the judge and the team of prosecutors walked in. The defendants, Bailey and Bates, heavily manacled, were led in. Bailey, permitted to buy clothing for the trial, wore a splendid double-breasted gray suit, black tie, and shining patent-leather shoes. His hair had been freshly cut, eliminating much of the graying hair around the temples. He looked very much like the businessman he had been in Chicago.

The prosecutors ignored the Shannons' confession that exonerated Bailey. Bates, who was told the governor of Oklahoma would personally see him in the electric chair if he stuck with his story that Bailey was not involved in the Urschel case, withdrew his statement. But when Urschel testified on three occasions that he had never heard Bailey's voice nor seen him in the brief time his blindfold was removed, the prosecutors became infuriated. Keenan, the assistant attorney general of the United States, stomped from the courtroom following Urschel's testimony. The bewildered Judge Vaught declared a five-minute recess until the fuming attorney could be brought back into the courtroom. Keenan had built a case around Urschel's fantastic memory. His observations were all keys to convicting the kidnappers. But Urschel's honesty in testifying was not something Keenan had planned on. It was a crippling blow to the prosecution and Keenan was irate.

Bailey had little to say during the twelve-day trial, resigned to the fact he was being railroaded. After the guilty verdict, the judge ordered the Kellys present at the sentencing, although they were yet to be tried. Every seat in the courtroom was filled as Judge Vaught stepped to the bench. A microphone had been set before the judge, the first time in federal court history this was done.

Kathryn Kelly suddenly rose to her feet.

"Your honor, sir," the red-haired woman said, "I plead not guilty." Kelly, who remained seated, was heard to mumble he too would plead not guilty. The crowd murmured at the unexpected and unorthodox presentation. Prosecutor Herbert K. Hyde, who had been promised by the Kellys they'd plead guilty, was stunned. Although their trial date had not been set, the Kellys had tossed a bombshell.

The judge instructed the court reporter to make the proper notation, then pounded the gavel for silence. He read a statement regarding the court's position on the law before passing sentence.

"I sentence the defendants Harvey Bailey, R. G. and Ora Shannon, and Albert Bates to life imprisonment. Armon Shannon is sentenced to ten years in the federal penitentiary, but sentence is suspended. Clifford Skelly and Edward Berman are sentenced to five years each."

Skelly and Berman had been charged with laundering the ransom money.

Bailey stood mute. Ora Shannon appeared on the verge of tears. Young Shannon muttered to himself while the judge lectured him about associating with his parents' friends in the future.

Newsmen rushed to telephones. Newsreel announcers jammed close for interviews. The judge again demanded silence. He announced the trial of the Kellys would begin the following Monday, October 9.

## The Good Ol' Boys

Following the Kingfisher job, Clark contacted the Bradys, and they spent some time together making the rounds in Tulsa. Although the depression was tearing most of the country apart, Tulsa—full of oil seekers, crooks, sharpies, and Indians—was in the midst of a boom.

Clark looked up Beulah Jackson, a young woman he'd met several years before at a barn dance in Muskogee. He was an expert square dancer and caller, and "Eula" loved to dance. Clark, like Bailey, felt women should be spared the life of a bank robber, and his itinerant status and time behind bars had not permitted him to see much of Miss Jackson. She was surprised and delighted to spend a couple of nights with her erstwhile dancing partner and Leona and Bob Brady.

At the noon meeting near Shawnee, Clark and Brady had agreed to join Bailey, in Brainerd, to case the bank. Saying good-bye to Tulsa and Miss Jackson for a while, Clark and the Bradys headed north in Brady's Ford sedan, a model whose front doors opened at the forward edge. Their trip was uneventful until they neared St. Cloud, Minnesota. They had stopped for a soft drink and were back on the road, Brady driving at his usual fast clip. Leona noticed her dress was caught in the door. She cracked the door slightly and tugged on the dress. The wind whipped the door from her grasp and peeled it back, slamming it into the rear of the car. The hinges were badly sprung and the door could not be closed properly. At the next town, a mechanic indicated repairs couldn't be made until the next day. They checked into a cottage court at the edge of town to spend the night.

After a hearty breakfast, they took the car to the shop. Clark became restless and walked across the street to pick up a newspaper. The headlines told the story of Bailey's capture in Paradise.

The trio returned to Tulsa after the door was repaired.

"It looks bad for old Harve," Brady said. "Maybe we ought to clear out of here for a spell."

Clark had felt for some time things were getting too hot in Oklahoma. He agreed a trip could prove beneficial in several ways. He phoned Eula and invited her to take a vacation trip to the Southwest along with the Bradys. She agreed readily and the trip was planned. Clark felt he needed a new car for the trek since the couples were going to travel separately.

"We better get a little traveling money," he suggested to Brady. They chose the Geary, Oklahoma, bank to provide the money and, with Underhill as the third man, hit the bank in early September. Clark bought a 1933 Plymouth coupe from the proceeds and the trip began.

Wilbur Underhill was upset by what he read in the McAlester *Democrat*.

"They're gonna stick the Old Man on the phony kidnap rap sure as hell," he muttered, throwing the newspaper against the wall. Despite a hatred for Bailey, he respected his talents as a bank robber. With Bailey put away, Underhill realized he'd have to plan his own jobs, which wasn't his forte. Brady and Clark had deserted Underhill because of his increasing enmity toward policemen, now bordering on outright insanity. Ed Davis and his wife had moved to Texas. Underhill was alone. He decided to return to the Cooksons and find Hazel Hudson.

Davis had resumed his bank-robbing career in central Texas, confining his activities to the small-town banks that one man could handle. The take was small, but it was a living. He became so adept at disappearing following a heist, lawmen began to refer to him as "the Fox." By September, 1933, he had amassed enough wealth to consider retirement. His wife had long envisioned living in California, and Davis decided the heat in the Midwest was too much. The Fox packed for California. The Bailey gang was defunct.

For a month, the Bradys, Clark, and Beulah enjoyed their vacation in Arizona. They dined well, rode horseback, hunted and fished and enjoyed the sun. In early October, they drove to Winslow, where Leona found some cottages far enough from the highway to be inconspicuous. Brady and Clark knew their pictures were in every post office in the country and had to remain on the alert, even in Arizona.

Big Bob indicated after several days that he was running short on cash. Clark agreed it was time to replenish their supply.

"Damn towns out here are too far apart, too much desert, too easy to set up roadblocks," Clark commented. "Maybe we ought to run back to Oklahoma."

"I cased a bank down in Frederick a couple years back," Brady agreed. "It's a one-horse town and the bank's only got one side door."

They informed the women they were making a quick trip and would be returning in a couple of days. The women knew better than to ask questions.

On the morning of October 6, 1933, Clark and Brady drove into the little town of Frederick. They had parked Clark's Plymouth coupe in a wooded area near Indiahoma, north of Frederick, and were using a new car they'd stolen at Carnegie, Oklahoma, a considerable distance away in order not to attract attention to the Frederick area. They needed someone to guard the side door during the robbery, so picked up a farm laborer, promising him $500 for the job. The three men entered the bank shortly after 9 a.m.

Clark entered first, followed by Brady and then the third man, who walked straight to the side door.

While Clark held his gun on the bank officials and two customers, Brady began stuffing money into a pillowcase. In minutes, he'd taken $5,000, but the bandits missed $15,000 more in cash in the tellers' cages and another $65,000 in the bank vault, which had a time lock. As they retreated, the bandits ordered banker P. R. Mounts, clerk Velma McKinley, and a customer, Hunter Harlan, to accompany them as hostages. Using the hostages as shields, the men drove first to the M-K-T depot, turned south a block, then east to Fourteenth Street and north to Highway 5. Undersheriff W. A. McAfee was called and he used the telephone in the Red Front Drug store to contact Sheriff Spence Akins's office, but the entire staff was making a liquor raid elsewhere in the county. The hostages were released unharmed once the bandits hit the edge of town. Several hours later, their abandoned car was found near

Indiahoma, where they'd switched back to Clark's car. The third man, never identified, was never seen again by Clark and Brady.

Inside the abandoned car, officers found a Conoco road map, a Clark trademark in that he preferred that company's free maps because they detailed more of the cat roads. The town of Frederick was circled in pencil.

Brady and Clark headed back to Winslow. The speedy Plymouth easily ate up the miles, and when they reached Amarillo, Texas, Brady decided to fill the tank before driving into the less-populated area further west. He searched for a Phillips 66 station. Brady's allegiance to the Oklahoma refining company was staunch. He never put any other kind of gasoline in his cars, even stolen ones. He finally located a station several blocks off the highway.

It was nearly dusk when Brady pulled into the station. An attendant pumped the tank full, then began wiping the windshield. For the first time, he noted Brady's face, with the scar beneath the left eye, the slightly twisted upper lip that curled into a semi-smile. The attendant, who had often visited the Amarillo jail to gawk at the prisoners, immediately recognized Brady. Back in September, 1931, when Brady was being returned to Oklahoma to face bank-robbing charges, he had been placed in the Amarillo jail overnight for safe-keeping. The youth at the filling station was one of the many pedestrians Brady had chatted with through the window bars. When Brady and Clark drove away, the attendant rushed to the telephone to call the police.

Clark had taken over the driving duties in Amarillo. The men cruised easily along Route 66, through the sparsely populated desert country where Texas and New Mexico meet. East of the New Mexico city of Tucumcari, Clark stopped at a hotel, where the pair ate a leisurely dinner. Again, Clark took the wheel, unaware that Amarillo police

had issued an all-points bulletin for Brady, possibly heading west. In Tucumcari, Sheriff Ira Allen and Deputy Ed
Jackson had been alerted. They set up a roadblock two
miles east of town. Highway crews were repairing the road
at night and the officers chose an area where warning flares
were set out. Clark spotted the flares as the Plymouth
topped a slight rise in the highway. He slammed on the
brakes and halted the car only feet away from a barrier
across the road. The sudden stop caused two shotguns on a
ledge behind the seat to tumble forward.

Three officers with flashlights surrounded the car, and
the occupants were ordered to get out. Clark remained
seated but Brady, putting on his salesman act, stepped onto
the pavement.

"Howdy, boys," Brady greeted the officers.

"We're looking for a stolen car," the sheriff announced.

"This ain't no stolen car," Clark replied, which was
true. He had bought the car, under the name of F. N. Atwood, and registered it in Wichita Falls, Texas, several
weeks before.

Clark reached for his registration certificate, but the
sheriff warned him not to put his hand in his pocket.

"Just get out," the officer repeated.

The officers began to shake down the pair, and when the
deputy found Brady's pockets full of cash, he yelled: "My
God, look at the money."

Brady then broke and ran. Sheriff Allen sent a blast of
shotgun pellets toward the fleeing man just as Deputy
Jackson fired his pistol. The shotgun blast tore into Brady's
back and sent him sprawling. He staggered to his feet and a
pistol bullet ripped into his left arm. Again, he fell into the
sagebrush, then rose and stumbled into the darkness.

The third officer grabbed Clark around the neck and re-
strained him.

The officers then put Clark in their car and prepared to
take him into Tucumcari.

"Hey, you can't leave that guy out there. He'll bleed to death," Clark protested.

"Listen, mister, we ain't going out in that desert at night looking for nobody. He'll be there in the morning, most likely."

At that instant, a Mexican who lived nearby ran up to them. He had heard shooting and said he'd stepped on a dead man in the brush. Sheriff Allen checked and found the badly wounded and unconscious Brady. Bleeding profusely, Brady would have died within minutes if the farmer had not stumbled across his body.

Clark was put in the Tucumcari jail and Brady was hospitalized. A guard was placed outside his room. The next day, October 7, Amarillo police arrived and promptly identified Brady but didn't recognize Clark. First reports indicated Brady's companion was Wilbur Underhill. Clark said his name was F. N. Atwood.

Clark insisted he didn't know Brady, claiming he was a hitch-hiker he'd picked up. When asked about the shotguns in the car, Clark said he was going hunting.

"Did you have to saw off the barrel to go hunting?" the officers wanted to know.

"Yeah, them blue quail out here really dart around," Clark insisted, fooling no one.

"Well, what are you doing with all that money?" the officers persisted.

"I made it hauling whiskey out of Juarez," Clark replied, the lie coming easily, since he had hauled whiskey—in 1927—from the Mexican city.

Clark and Brady were fingerprinted and their identity ascertained when the FBI checked the prints. They were taken to Santa Fe for safekeeping. Despite his terrible wounds, Brady was placed in a cell in a basement area behind the prison's electric chair. Clark was put in death row with twenty-two men awaiting execution.

Kansas authorities were notified to retrieve the pair as

soon as Brady was able to travel. On October 15, Guard Jack Sherman, one of the hostages in the Memorial Day escape, arrived with Charley Lindsey, the elderly head of the twine shop, to return the escapees. The four men returned to Kansas aboard the "Santa Fe Chief," a crack train of the day, disembarking at Holiday, Kansas, just outside Kansas City. The final miles to Lansing were completed by motor car.

Clark and Brady were assigned to the special blockhouse for dangerous or escape-prone prisoners. They were placed in a maximum-security cellblock inside a concrete building surrounded by a wall within the main prison confines.

Now only Underhill and Davis remained at large before the state of Kansas could clear the books.

## The Death of the Killer

# 15

The director of the Kansas Crime Bureau, O. P. Ray, was under pressure. Of the eleven escapees, the two most dangerous, Underhill and Davis, were still at large. Governor Alf Landon had ordered Ray to "spare no expense" in finding the two convicted murderers. So Ray ordered a special armored car to be used in the hunt, and assigned twenty men to the case. They left for Tulsa in early November, 1933.

Underhill was now being called "the Southwest Executioner" by the avid press, always seeking catch-phrases for the badmen. Director Ray decided to concentrate on him first.

The twenty special officers enlisted the help of federal agents and Oklahoma state officers. They scoured the Cookson Hills, but, like most before them, turned up nothing. Incredibly, while officers were quizzing the local residents, Underhill walked into the courthouse in Coalgate, Oklahoma, and applied for a marriage license using his real name. He walked out unrecognized. The incident sent the attorney general's office in Washington, D. C., into a rage. R. H. Colvin, the crack agent who had led the Urschel kidnapping investigation, was immediately assigned to the Underhill case, since the government still felt Underhill was involved in the Union Station massacre. Underhill and his bride, Hazel Hudson, were swallowed up again by the hills as the federal agents swarmed into the southern tier of counties around Coalgate, well outside the Cookson Hills boundaries.

Underhill made another stupid blunder, but, again, incredibly, got away with it. He gave the clergyman who performed the wedding ceremony the address of Hazel's house in Oklahoma City, with the request that the marriage certificate be mailed there when it was returned from the state offices. The minister informed law officers, and Colvin assigned a man to watch the house. When the newlyweds arrived in the middle of the night a week later, the agent drove to the nearest phone to notify Colvin. By the time he returned, the Underhills had gone, stopping only long enough to pick up their mail—and the marriage certificate.

He had another close call when two carloads of armed lawmen descended on a farm near Konowa, having heard he was there. As they drove to the farm on a narrow dirt road, they pulled to one side to let an approaching car pass. In the car were Wilbur and Hazel. By the time the officers turned their autos around in the narrow roadway, the Underhills were miles away. Wilbur, who had been ill, was en route to town to visit a doctor and was not aware the officers were closing in until he saw them in the cars.

Underhill had spent most of the summer and fall of 1933 on the run. He robbed a bank in Canton, in north central Oklahoma, on July 5, two days after the Clinton robbery, but the loot was less than expected. After the gang's Kingfisher robbery, he joined Clark and Brady to rob the bank in Geary. He took part in a job at Baxter Springs, Kansas, on October 6, then picked off banks at Galena, Kansas, and Stuttgart, Arkansas, before returning to Oklahoma to test the Harrah First National Bank, aided by Jack Lloyd and Ralph Roe, old friends of his. When they were scared off of the Harrah job, Underhill drove to Coalgate, where a month earlier he'd applied for the wedding license. He stuck up the bank there on December 13.

Underhill and his bride, who stuffed her brassiere with bills from the robberies, hid out in the Vian, Oklahoma, vicinity for a couple of weeks to let the persistent Department of Justice officers cool a bit. They stayed there with friends of Charley Cotner, alias "Cotton," who had shared some of the recent robberies with Underhill. During that time, Wilbur's mother and his sister Dorothy drove to Vian from Kansas City one weekend. Wilbur extracted twenty dollars from his wife's brassiere to give to his mother. Underhill was not a generous man.

The day after Christmas, the Underhills drove to Shawnee, where they rented a small, two-bedroom stucco house at 606 West Dewey Street. Ralph Roe, wanted in Ardmore, Oklahoma, for an automobile accident, and on parole from the state penitentiary, lived with them.

Hazel had pleaded with Underhill to go straight, and he had told her he would. But first he wanted to unload $5,300 in bonds of the Franklin, Kentucky, Title & Trust Company. He made an appointment in Oklahoma City with a fence. Wilbur rose about 3 a.m. on December 30 to make the trip. Hazel dressed first and made coffee on the chilly morning. Roe was still asleep in his room along with a young beauty operator, Eva Mae Nichols of Seminole, Oklahoma, working in Shawnee.

Acting on a tip, twenty-four officers from the Department of Justice, Oklahoma state patrol, and Shawnee police department quietly surrounded the house on Dewey

Street. A single lighted window cracked the darkness. R. H. Colvin peered in below a drawn shade that came within an inch of the sill. Underhill was in his underwear, standing in the center of the room, and Hazel was seated on the bed, fully clothed. On a bureau against the wall was a Luger pistol.

Colvin returned to his fellow officers.

"We've got to take him now, he's getting ready to leave," the agent whispered. "Let's go."

Colvin and Agent Frank Smith, a survivor of the Union Station massacre, moved to the window.

Although the night air was cold, the window had been opened about two inches at the bottom. Colvin put his lips close to the opening and shouted: "Stick 'em up, Wilbur. We're the law."

Underhill whirled, grabbed the Luger off the bureau, and ran out of the bedroom. Colvin and Smith retreated and gave the order to fire. Twenty-four guns began blasting the cottage. The officers used rifles, pistols, and shotguns to bombard the house from four sides. Bullets plowed into the walls, shattered the windows, and ripped the curtains to shreds. Underhill returned a few shots aimlessly. Roe and his girl friend jumped to their feet at the first shots, then retreated to a closet. A rifle slug tore into the room and struck the young woman in the mid-section, blood gushing from the wound in spurts. She collapsed to the floor, twisting in pain, and then passed out.

Underhill, in his underwear and barefooted, stood by the front door of the now-darkened house, the bedroom light having been shot out by the first blast of gunfire. He paused for a moment, grabbed the door knob, and leaped onto the porch. He began running across the yard, bullets peppering the bushes on both sides of him. He ran about ten feet before the first bullet ripped into his shoulder, sending him crashing to the ground. He rolled over and came up running. A second bullet tore into his other shoulder, then a third and yet a fourth. Somehow, he kept on his feet. He reached the street, and a cornfield offered shelter on the other side. Just as he reached the first protecting stalks, a fifth bullet struck him in the head. Miraculously, the bullet glanced off his skull and he continued running. As he thrashed through the field, the sound of the officers giving chase spurred him to superhuman effort, and he soon outdistanced his pursuers. On and on he ran, aimlessly at first, then struggling to reach a building in the downtown area that was a criminal hangout, fronting as a used-furniture store. For sixteen blocks, barefooted and clad only in underwear on a cold December night and with eleven bullet holes in his body, the crazed Underhill ran before reaching the store. He smashed into the back door, stumbled toward a display bed in the store window, and dropped exhausted onto the mattress.

Sheriff Stanley Rogers, who arrived too late to take part in the shooting barrage, led the searching party. He reasoned that eventually Underhill would turn up in daylight at the furniture store, so went to the downtown area to place a guard. He was totally shocked to find the unconscious Underhill already there, blood oozing from wounds in various parts of his body. Positive Underhill was going to die momentarily, Rogers ordered him taken to the Shawnee Municipal Hospital.

Hazel escaped unharmed in the barrage, but Roe and his girl friend were wounded badly. They were rushed to the hospital, where attendants indicated the girl could not live through the day.

The wire services told the nation about the unbelievable sixteen-block run. Underhill's mother and sister drove in from Kansas City the next day, hoping to arrive in time to hear Wilbur's last words. Within forty-eight hours, Underhill was able to hold a press interview.

"Actually, I only got hit five times, but them shots made eleven holes in me," he laughingly informed the astounded reporters. "I counted each one as they hit me. When I set sail, they sure poured it to me."

Clarence Sowers, a Wichita lawyer who had defended Underhill in the killing of Officer Merle Colver in 1931, visited with his client. When he left the room, reporters ganged around.

"He will die," Sowers confided, "but he doesn't think so. He's got a hole in his belly about where the appendix is that looks like a deer rifle or large-caliber rifle slug hit him. It's about the size of a half-dollar and the slug went clean through him close to the spine."

Meanwhile, Eva Mae Nichols died from her wound. Her dying wish, according to an undertaker's wife, Mrs. J. C. Chadwick, who heard the girl's request, was to be buried exactly at sunset in the Maple Grove Cemetery in Seminole. Services were held at the First Methodist Church in Seminole the next day, with burial exactly at sunset.

Wilbur's brother Earl, recently released from prison, was on the WPA payroll in Joplin and had gone to Pittsburg, Kansas, to visit his estranged wife when news of Wilbur's capture reached him. However, he couldn't get to the hospital because his wife had him thrown in jail on a vagrancy charge, following a dispute. Wilbur's other brother, Ernest, was still doing time in the Missouri State Penitentiary for the 1913 murder. But Almira Underhill and dependable Dorothy kept a vigil beside the bed of the wounded badman.

Amazingly, Underhill began to recover. Doctors were astounded by his will to live. In Oklahoma City, the governor's office could hardly believe the reports, yet ordered Underhill transported to the state prison at McAlester immediately, lest some of his friends attempt to free him from the poorly guarded hospital. Although Underhill was still on the critical list, less than a week after the shooting, officers lifted him into an ambulance for the hundred-mile ride. As Underhill was being carried into the prison hospital, Dr. J. A. Munn, the prison physician, stated that the prisoner could not survive his wounds. Shortly after, on January 6, 1934, Underhill died in the prison hospital. Reports circulated immediately, which were denied by prison officials, that Underhill was beaten with clubs once inside the walls.

"Wilbur was trying to go straight," the bereaved widow exclaimed, "but they just wouldn't leave him alone."

Underhill was buried on January 10, a cold, gray day. The body had arrived in Joplin by train and more than a thousand curious onlookers watched the gray metal casket being unloaded. The body was taken to the home of a sister, Mrs. Anna Lewis. Friends of the family were allowed to pay their final respects to the outlaw, but the morbidly curious were locked out.

When the Reverend C. P. Mills of the Byers Avenue Methodist Church, where Wilbur had attended Sunday school as a youth, began the funeral services, several hundred people jammed their way into the foyer and had to be forcibly removed.

Seated in the pews reserved for the family were Ernest, who had been given a furlough from prison; Earl, released from the Pittsburg, Kansas, jail; and Almira Underhill and her daughters, Dorothy Underhill, Margaret Smith, Grace Baine, and Anna Lewis.

Pastor Mills intoned his prayers from the pulpit and concluded his sermon with these words: "Man cannot tamper with the laws of any realm of life without expecting to be broken by those same laws."

The funeral cortege moved to the Ozark Memorial Park Cemetery, where parked cars lined the streets. Despite the cold, it was the largest funeral in the city's history. The Joplin *Globe* estimated the crowd in excess of two thousand. The tombstone properly identified Underhill as "Wilber" instead of his chosen spelling of the name.

# Over the Wall—Again

# 16

With Bailey incarcerated and Underhill dead, the FBI chalked off the Bailey-Underhill gang. Pretty Boy Floyd had been neutralized somewhat by the intense pressure applied by Oklahoma and Kansas state officers. Kansas, concentrating on the remaining free Memorial Day escapee, Ed Davis, continued to use its twenty-man strike force inside Oklahoma, following special authorization by Governor Murray. The special force, coupled with Oklahoma's troops, had been enough to drive Floyd from his haunts in the Cooksons. He fled to Ohio, where he had relatives. When Dillinger's presence brought attention to the area, Floyd left for the relatively safer Tulsa area. He was no longer making headlines.

The emergence of a new folk anti-hero was now the dominant concern for the Department of Justice. John Herbert Dillinger, bank robber and murderer, had sprung into prominence in mid-1933. On June 10, he joined Bill Shaw and Paul Parker to heist the National Bank of New Carlisle, Indiana. Then, he joined with Harry Copeland to stick up the Daleville, Indiana, bank in July, and followed with the First National Bank of Montpelier, Indiana, in August. On August 18, the pair hit the bank at Bluffton, Ohio, which proved to be a turning point in the career of the man who would soon become the new symbol of the depression-era bank robbers.

Uneasily, the FBI watched Dillinger's activities, although until September 6, 1933, the Indianan had not made a major score. On that day, he joined with Copeland and Hilton Crouch to hit the Massachusetts Avenue State Bank of Indianapolis for $25,000. This set off a detailed search and Dillinger was picked up in Dayton, Ohio, two weeks later. He was hustled to the Lima, Ohio, jail to await trial for the Bluffton job.

Dillinger had served time in the Indiana state prison at Michigan City from July, 1929, until May 22, 1933, when he was paroled. While behind the walls, he had been tutored in the art of bank robbing by Harry Pierpont, Charles Makley, Russell Clark, and John Hamilton, experienced pros. Those four, along with six others—Ed Shouse, Joe Burns, Walt Dietrich, Jim Jenkins, Joe Fox, and Jim Clark (not related to the Jim Clark previously mentioned)—broke out of the Michigan City facility. On September 26, Dillinger predicted to fellow inmates in Lima that his buddies would soon free him. On October 12, Pierpont, Makley, Russell Clark, Hamilton, and Shouse walked into the Lima jail, gunned down Sheriff Jess Sarber, and sprung their erstwhile companion. From then on, Dillinger was headline material—and he reveled in it. The Dillinger-led gang was now ready for big time. They knocked off the Central National Bank of Greencastle, Indiana, for $75,000 on October 23, then followed with the American Bank & Trust in Racine, Wisconsin, on November 20. They laid low the rest of 1933.

While the Dillinger gang was moving to the top of the publicity heap, the Barker-Karpis outfit was honing its own techniques. Bank robbing was becoming more dangerous with the federals now involved, so Freddy and Dock Barker and Karpis got into the business of kidnapping for ransom. Although nothing new in the field of crime, the tactic was refined by the huge Barker-Karpis combine. Their first victim was William A. Hamm, Jr., a St. Paul brewery owner. The snatch was made two days before the Union Station affair in Kansas City, and the events combined to shake the public attitude toward criminals. Now crime was getting personal, not just institutional. The mass murder in Kansas City was a stunning and sobering event. And even though Hamm was released unharmed upon payment of $100,000 ransom, the Barkers, Karpis, and their fellow kidnappers, Charley Fitzgerald, Freddy Goetz, and Monty Bolton, had fouled their nest.

Then, the gang really did themselves in with the public and the Department of Justice when they killed a policeman while robbing the Swift & Company payroll of $30,000 in South St. Paul, Minnesota, on August 15. For the rest of the year, the gang retired.

As 1934 began, the FBI watched and waited for the two major gangs to resume action. They didn't have long to wait.

On January 15, the First National Bank of East Chicago, Indiana, was robbed and a policeman killed. Although there was considerable conjecture by the press that Dillinger and his boys were not involved in the heist, the FBI concluded they were the culprits. Dillinger, Clark, Makley, and Pierpont fled to Arizona. Fire broke out in their hotel, and firemen became suspicious of the weight of two suitcases found in their room. Several pistols were discovered inside, and the four men and their women companions were arrested. Dillinger was extradited to Indiana to stand trial for the East Chicago killing, the others to Ohio for the murder of Sheriff Sarber at Lima. Dillinger was put in the escape-proof, modern Crown Point, Indiana, jail.

Simultaneously, the Barker-Karpis combine returned to action. On January 19, Freddy and Dock Barker, Karpis, Volney Davis, Fred Goetz, Bill Weaver, Larry DeVol, and Harry Campbell kidnapped Edward G. Bremer, a Minneapolis banker, demanding $200,000 ransom. They moved to the head of the FBI's most-wanted list.

In the meantime, Harvey Bailey was having problems in the federal penitentiary at Leavenworth. Even his arrival was unusual. Bailey and Bates were flown by Ford tri-motor airplane from Oklahoma City to Leavenworth, officials cautiously aware of what happened in the Frank Nash transfer. From the beginning, the convicted kidnappers were treated differently from other inmates. They were placed in solitary confinement in a special section of the prison known as "the Annex," where the most dangerous and degenerate prisoners were held. Bailey and Bates were not allowed tobacco or reading material. To protest this infringement of their rights, they went on a hunger strike. Prison officials force-fed them a gallon of milk each day, a pint at a time, by inserting a rubber hose through the nostrils.

When they persisted in their protest, the two new "fish" were told that a maximum-security facility for the incorrigibles, the escape-prone, and "special cases"—the new federal penitentiary on Alcatraz, an island in San Francisco Bay—was nearly ready for occupancy. Bailey and Bates believed they'd be among the first arrivals regardless of their behavior at Leavenworth, so continued to demand equal treatment.

Sheriff Smoot Schmid of Dallas visited Bailey in an attempt to get details about the Tom Manion case. Manion, the deputy who aided Bailey in his escape from the Dallas jail, and his friend, Grover Bevill, had been sentenced for aiding the escape and were already in Leavenworth. But Schmid wanted to hear Bailey's version of the incident. Although convinced Manion would have shot him had he used the front door of the Dallas jail, Bailey wouldn't reveal how the pistol and hacksaw blade got under his mattress. Shortly after Schmid's visit, Attorney General Cummings called on Bailey. He offered to permit Bailey to remain at Leavenworth and eventually gain parole if he'd reveal certain details about the Capone mob in Chicago, the hot-money market in Minneapolis, the Lincoln, Nebraska, bank robbery that remained such a mystery to lawmen, and the St. Valentine's Day and Union Station massacres. The alternative for not talking—Alcatraz!

Bailey's silence didn't surprise the attorney general.

"I figured as much," he said, turning to leave the cell. As an afterthought, he looked at Bailey and smiled.

"See you on Alcatraz."

Kansas prison officials put Clark and Brady into isolation upon their return from New Mexico. A building surrounded by a ten-foot-high wall, and located about twenty yards from the main cell house, served as the isolation unit. It was referred to as "Number Two," and only the tougher inmates or those with escape records were assigned there. In essence, Lansing's isolation unit was a prison within a prison with its own kitchen facilities and rotating guards. A two-tiered affair, the building was cold most of the winter and like an oven in the summer. It was November when Brady and Clark arrived, and Brady was still in considerable pain from the wounds he received in New Mexico.

There was a single window on the east side, and Clark could see Tower 3½, the guard post atop the wall right on the third-base line of the baseball diamond in the recreation yard. By carefully noting each dusk the position of the dipper in the guard's water bucket, the chair, and even the broom in the corner, and ascertaining the next morning they were in the same place, Clark determined there was no guard in the tower from dusk to dawn. Warden Lacey Simpson, in an economy move, had the post vacated at night.

Clark also studied the habits of the guards assigned within the unit. He knew some waited until after the sixteen or so inmates were finished with breakfast before they ate. Two attendants from the kitchen brought breakfast each morning about 6:15, and two inmates were let out to distribute the trays to the others.

One of the guards was a 300-pound Osage Indian named Clyde Deer. He often teased Clark and Brady about the Memorial Day break, claiming that had he been on duty that day, they'd not have escaped. Clark vowed that when he did make a second break, it'd be on Deer's shift.

"Then we'll see just how tough he is," Clark told Brady.

Clark assessed the situation. Any attempt would have to be made before 7 a.m., when the sun first appeared in January in that part of the country, and it would have to be during Deer's shift, at a time when Clark and Brady were working the kitchen detail together. Other details such as overpowering the guard and scaling the outer wall were as yet unsolved.

The prison grapevine had already passed the word Clark was planning another break. Billie Woods and Cliff Dopson immediately set about getting transferred to the isolation ward so they could join in. Woods clobbered another convict and was slapped into isolation on January 15. Dopson did the same and with the same result. Fred Cody, another Oklahoman, was working in the twine plant and wanted to be in on the break. He punched a fellow inmate and was sent to isolation only to have Charley Lindsey, the twine-plant supervisor, use influence and have him returned. This time, Cody hit a black inmate over the head with a stillson wrench to get back in isolation. Benny Young and

Tommy McMahan, already in isolation in screened cells on bread and water, said they would go, too, as did Charles McArthur, who used the alias "Claude Newton." Frank Delmar, another Oklahoma bank robber and a close friend of Clark's, had been sentenced on a second-degree murder charge for killing Ernie Gough, a Leavenworth city detective, in 1932. Delmar declared his intent to join the group. Thus, the manpower problem was solved.

The remaining problem was getting over the twenty-five-foot limestone outer wall. Three tom cats and two canaries helped solve that obstacle.

One isolation inmate was a bird fancier. Prison officials let him have a couple of canaries. Outside the building was a locked shed in which used lumber and baling wire were stored. The shed had a tarpaper roof that perpetually leaked, and a twelve-foot ladder was kept handy to allow access to repair the roof. Three stray cats, which the inmates named "Monk," "Skinny," and "Spot," used the shed as a home. They were cared for by an inmate named "Cap" Lee, who fed them with scraps from the meals. Clark convinced the bird lover that he could construct better cages for the canaries if he had some baling wire. The guards okayed the use of the wire for that purpose, and in the ensuing weeks, Clark managed to hide a dozen strands under the lumber. When snow and ice made it impossible for the cats to reach a small window where they entered the shed, Clark suggested that a couple of long boards be placed at an angle to the window so the cats could walk into the aperture.

"Them damn cats howl all night when they can't get in," Clark told the guards. Permission to put up the boards was given. Now Clark had the twelve-foot ladder and two ten-foot boards that could be used as extensions to top the twenty-five-foot wall. Clark figured the pair of two-by-sixes could be fastened to the ladder with the baling wire, eliminating any need for hammering. Less than twenty feet from the building was a small room that guards going on duty used for their morning coffee, and Clark felt noise emanating from the shed could be heard. The wire could also be used to add rungs to the extension, thus producing the longer ladder they needed.

On Friday morning, January 19, all conditions were "go." Deer was on duty, Clark and Brady had the kitchen detail, and it was pitch dark outside at 6 a.m. The two kitchen helpers arrived with the breakfast trays, and the guard unlocked Brady and Clark. A prison barber unexpectedly arrived but sat down to wait until breakfast was over. Deer began eating his breakfast while the trays were being passed under the cell doors.

"Hey, Deer, gimme the keys and I'll give these boys some milk. This pitcher won't go under the door," Clark yelled to the guard, who handed over his ring of keys without looking up from his tray.

Clark unlocked the cells of Dopson, Young, McMahan, Delmar, McArthur, and Cody. Woods was in another section, watching quietly as the freed inmates rushed toward the unsuspecting guard. Brady grabbed him around the neck.

"Let out one yelp and you're a dead man," Brady growled. The helpless guard, the two attendants, and the barber were tossed into a cell and Clark turned the lock.

Brandishing the guard's club, Clark looked toward the cell.

"One word and you guys have had it," he warned.

The freed convicts ran to the back door of the cellblock while Dopson ran to release Woods. He couldn't find the right key and began to bang on the steel door with a hammer he had found in the guard's desk.

"That crazy bastard is going to get us caught," Delmar yelled. "Let's get moving."

The building had a rear door, and as the convicts ran toward it, Clark spotted a hose used to wash down the cellblocks.

"Grab that and we'll tie it to the ladder to help us down the outside," he instructed one of the others. Silently, the men eased into the early morning darkness and slipped inside the shed. They hurriedly began wiring the addition to the ladder. It took almost thirty minutes to complete the job. Dopson could still be heard banging on his friend's cell door, but miraculously, none of the guards noticed it. Trusties were being assembled for work outside the walls in the mines and at the dairy farm, and their noise muffled much of the pounding.

It was nearly dawn by the time the ladder was ready.

"Let's make a run for it, boys," Brady said. "Me and Frank will carry it, and the minute it hits the wall, you guys start climbing."

Stealthily, the seven convicts edged around the shed, then broke toward the wall. The lights atop the walls outlined the running men. Several hundred yards away, a guard had opened a small gate to allow the trusties out. When they saw the running men, realizing there'd be gunfire, the trusties began running. The guard in Tower 4 then saw the gang with the ladder, and fired a shot. In Tower 3 at the southeast corner of the yard, a guard was literally caught with his pants down. He was using the toilet when he heard the shot fired, but it was some time before he could get into position to use his rifle.

The convicts scampered up the ladder. McArthur was the first to go over the wall. The hose wasn't long enough to reach the ground, and when McArthur dropped the final six feet onto the frozen cinders below, his ankle snapped. The others made the drop without injury and scattered in all directions. There were no lights shining outside the wall, and the men, including McArthur, disappeared in the darkness. Clark and Delmar ran east and then southward toward a gulley that led into a cornfield. Brady, Young, Cody, and McMahan ran straight south, while McArthur hobbled off to the east of the prison.

Despite the hail of bullets, none of the escapees was hit.

Cody's wristwatch chain was clipped by a bullet, and McMahan, the last one over, had seven bullet holes in his clothes. The ladder was pulverized.

Clark and Delmar ran for about thirty minutes before coming to a gravel road. The sun was breaking over the hills to the east and helped boost the 24-degree temperature a bit. Clark had to stop once to remove fourteen dollars he put in the toe of his right shoe prior to the break.

It was nearly eight o'clock when a black Plymouth coupe driven by Lewis S. Dresser, a twenty-six-year-old schoolteacher, approached. Clark stepped to the middle of the road and raised his right hand. Dresser pulled to a stop and rolled down his car window.

"I'm trying to get to Kansas City," Clark said, moving toward the open window.

"Hell, you're going the wrong way," Dresser advised.

"You know, I thought I was turned around," Clark smiled, reaching for the car door handle. He whipped open the Plymouth's door and moved behind the wheel, shoving Dresser to the center seat. Delmar got in the other side. Clark directed the car south, once more heading for Oklahoma.

When the trio hit the outskirts of Bonner Springs, Clark was fearful the busy bridge crossing the Kaw would be guarded. He was relieved to see no one there. He hit the bridge going almost seventy miles per hour, and the board flooring rattled noisily. Once across the bridge, Clark noted the car was nearly out of gasoline.

"Where in the hell's the closest station?" Clark asked Dresser.

"About a mile and a half down the road, but they know me around here," the schoolteacher replied.

"We don't care none about that," Delmar said. "Gimme your overcoat." As Delmar slipped into Dresser's coat to hide his denim uniform, Clark put on the teacher's hat. They pulled into the station driveway. The attendant recognized Dresser but never suspected anything was amiss.

As the Plymouth sped toward the Oklahoma line, Dresser became worried about his car. He told Clark not to speed. The Oklahoman laughed.

"Mister, I ain't gonna hurt your car. You keep quiet and we'll get along fine. You've got a lot of sitting to do, so take it easy."

Meanwhile, Brady and his bunch spent the day hiding in a cornfield. That night they walked along country roads despite temperatures that dropped into the high teens. On Saturday, they hid in a ravine. They had nothing to eat since their hurried breakfast on Friday.

As Ed Davis drove along Route 66, he pondered his future. He glanced at his sleeping wife alongside him and wondered if a new life in California was the answer. Bank robbing was getting more precarious, and the gangs like the Barkers and Dillingers and the insane antics of Clyde Barrow and Bonnie Parker had everybody looking for criminals. The Fox looked at his arms as he drove along, wondering if there was any way to remove the identifying tattoos. On his left arm was a rose-colored horseshoe surrounding a woman's head in red and black. Below that was a horse's head and a girl in close-fitting tights. Near the wrist was another woman's head and bust. On the inside of the left arm was a dagger, a cowgirl, and the name "Lon" indelibly stenciled. There were more tattoos on his right arm, a total of sixteen decorations in all.

Davis sighed heavily. He'd made up his mind. He was going straight in California.

# The Beginning of the End

# 17

J. Edgar Hoover called his favorite agent, Melvin Purvis, to the Washington, D. C., offices of the FBI. Purvis, who reported directly to the chief, was given the special assignment of tracking down the Barkers, Karpis, and Floyd. Dillinger, being held in the Crown Point, Indiana, jail, was apparently of no current concern to the bureau. Bonnie and Clyde were being hounded by every law officer in the Southwest, so the FBI had only cursory interest in them. The prison break in Kansas was of some concern since Brady and Clark were once again on the loose, but temporarily, at least, Hoover wanted to concentrate on the Barkers, Karpis, and Floyd.

In Topeka, Governor Landon called Major Smith to his office, as before.

"Wint, I want those men back in Lansing in three days. Do what you have to to get them back. The Kansas Bankers Association is all over me with Clark and Brady out again," the governor instructed Smith.

The break on January 19 mystified everyone with its execution. Clark was credited with developing the plot when the nine inmates who chose not to go told most of what they knew. Officials never learned of Dopson's part in the escape since he returned to his cell when he couldn't get Woods's door open.

The first of the escapees was recaptured in Kansas City, Kansas, on Saturday, the day following the break. The injured McArthur was picked up, his ankle severely broken. Doctors marveled at his ability to walk on it. Then, on Sunday morning, the schoolteacher was released by Delmar and Clark. Clark had driven first to Harrah, where he hoped a friend would hide them, but the man had moved. He then drove to Muskogee but found another empty house. So he drove to Pawhuska, where Goldie Johnson, a girl friend, had been keeping Clark's car (the Plymouth coupe he was driving when picked up in Tucumcari). Early Sunday morning he pulled into Goldie's yard, but he pulled right out again when she ran from the house to warn him there was a patrol car parked nearby. Goldie waited for a phone call, then delivered the car to Clark near Nelagoney, a small town nearby. Clark gave Dresser his car, his coat and hat, and a five-dollar bill for gasoline back home, with the warning that he was not to report to police until he arrived in Bartlesville.

"Mister, I'll drive all the way home before I tell anybody," the relieved teacher replied. Although he did notify police in Bartlesville, it made little difference to Clark and Delmar, already in Tulsa.

Brady and his companions were having terrible luck. They prowled a farmhouse and managed to get some food and an old pump shotgun, but had to return to the brush during the day. They hid by day and walked by night in subfreezing temperatures, hungry most of the time.

On January 22, after walking nearly forty miles in the three days since the escape, the exhausted convicts deserted the woods at 1:30 p.m. to raid a farmhouse nearby. The four denim-clad fugitives were spotted crossing the field, and the sheriff's office was notified. Undersheriff Harve Lininger, thinking the men might be hunters from Missouri, possibly without licenses, grabbed Deputy Ed Schlotman and drove nine miles southeast of Paola to the Henry Kohlenberg farm.

Schlotman carried a sawed-off shotgun. Lininger spotted the men crossing a fence into the Charles McCoy pasture. He stopped the car near the men and got out.

"What are you doing?" the undersheriff inquired.

"Not much," Brady responded, hiding the stolen shotgun under his jacket.

"What's your name, buddy?"

"None of your damned business," Brady replied.

Suddenly, Brady whipped the gun to his shoulder and pulled the trigger. The old piece clicked but there was no explosion. He began working frantically to free the jammed shell in the chamber. Lininger drew his pistol and fired four times. Brady staggered, dropped the shotgun, grabbed his middle, and then fell to his knees. Deputy Schlotman fired his shotgun and Brady toppled to the ground. Incredibly, he arose and began to stagger away, but Lininger emptied his pistol in Brady's direction. With the last volley, Brady's body jerked violently and fell to the ground. At last Big Bob Brady was dead.

Their ammunition gone, the officers ran to the car as the remaining three convicts fled to some woods nearby. Lininger drove to the McCoy farm and phoned the sheriff's office. Captain Walter Ringer of the National Guard was notified. Although the guard units at Olathe, Ottawa, Lawrence, Kansas City, Fort Scott, Atchison, and Pleasanton had been called out to search for the escapees, the Paola troop had not. Captain Ringer, however, drove to the Kohlenberg farm and spotted the remaining convicts about five hundred yards east of the house. They began waving their hands above the heads, and the captain had no trouble taking them prisoner. Seconds later, a car full of law officers arrived and handcuffed the convicts.

In Paola, a crowd gathered around the jail as the prisoners were brought in. Immediately, the jail telephone began to ring as reports of the capture reached reporters in Kansas City. At first, the convicts remained mute, but later they admitted they were Benjamin Young, twenty, Tommy McMahan, twenty-one, and Fred Cody, thirty-three. Brady's body was taken to the Metzler Funeral Home. Despite all the shots fired, Brady had taken only two shotgun pellets in the heart area, several in the head, and one ball from Lininger's pistol. That shot had pierced the abdomen and exited from the left side. More than 2,500 people queued up to view the corpse at the funeral home the following day. The body was shipped to Ada, Oklahoma, for burial. Major Smith arrived from Topeka along with several troopers to return the prisoners to Lansing. One of the troopers was Ed Arn, who would much later become governor of Kansas. Smith, who would later become a United States congressman, now set his sights on Jim Clark and Frank Delmar.

On March 3, 1934, John Dillinger roared back into headlines all over the world. He carved a pistol from the wooden part of a small washboard provided prisoners in the Crown Point, Indiana, jail, daubed it with bootblack, and fooled a guard into relinquishing his keys. Taking several machine guns, Dillinger and Herbert Youngblood, a black inmate awaiting trial for murder, stole Sheriff Lillian Holley's personal car and escaped. Dillinger ran the cat roads to Illinois and therefore, in violating the Dyer Act by crossing a state line in a stolen car, for the first time became eligible for federal prosecution.

The timing of Dillinger's break was inopportune, to say the least, for the FBI. When J. Edgar Hoover heard of the escape, he became livid. The Department of Justice had authored nine bills for Congress aimed at the fight against crime, and any reflection against any law enforcement agency might hurt the cause, Hoover felt. Although Dillinger's escape was from a county jail, Hoover felt it was possible some congressmen or the general public might associate the break with the federal force. Actually the escape pushed Congress into action and all nine bills were passed, thus assuring the FBI sufficient funding and new tools for the battle against crime. With the new bills, it became a federal offense to assault or kill a federal officer, to rob a national bank, to flee across state lines to avoid prosecution, to transport stolen property over a state line if the value was more than $5,000, to use interstate communications in extortion attempts, and to take hostages or kidnap victims over a state line. Furthermore, agents were allowed to carry weapons at all times and given full police powers throughout the nation. Hoover's long-requested changes were signed into law by President Franklin D. Roosevelt in June, 1934.

Dillinger holed up in Chicago and began rounding up a new gang. With Pierpont, Makley, and Clark behind bars, only John Hamilton of the old group was available. Homer Van Meter became Dillinger's right-hand man, although a young punk named Lester Gillis, who preferred to be known as "Baby Face" Nelson, wanted to run the show. Eddie Green and Tommy Carroll became additional members of the mob. Three days after the escape from Crown Point, Dillinger and his new boys robbed the Security National Bank of Sioux Falls, South Dakota. The gun-happy Nelson shot a policeman as the gang netted nearly $50,-000. Ten days later, they struck again, hitting the First National Bank of Mason City, Iowa, for $52,000. A number of shots were fired, and Dillinger and Hamilton each received minor gunshot wounds, as did two citizens. Dillinger and Hamilton fled to St. Paul to get their wounds treated.

While nursing the injuries, the gang decided to lie low at

a closed fishing resort near Rhinelander, Wisconsin. The lodge "Little Bohemia" was not scheduled to open until May, but the bar was open for a few cold-weather fishermen and workers from the nearby Civilian Conservation Corps camp.

In Chicago, Melvin Purvis picked up a tip about the gang's whereabouts. He rounded up dozens of agents from the various offices and converged on the lodge on April 22, 1934.

As the agents slipped into the underbrush and thick woods surrounding the lodge, three CCC workers who had stopped by for a beer exited and walked toward their car. Mistakenly believing it was the gang taking its leave, the agents opened fire. By the time Purvis halted the shooting, one of the CCC men, Eugene Boiseneau, lay dead. Naturally, the firing tipped off the gang inside. Dillinger, Van Meter, Hamilton, and Carroll fled out the back door. Nelson, in a cabin outside the main lodge with his wife, escaped into the woods. In the ensuing chase, an FBI agent was killed. The FBI was humiliated by the fiasco and Hoover again went wild in Washington. He appointed Agent Samuel Cowley to the task of tracking down Dillinger regardless of the methods necessary. A $10,000 reward was posted on Dillinger's head, dead or alive, and five states affected by his raids put up another $10,000.

The public interest in Dillinger was equal to any criminal chase in history. The newspapers, caught up in the excitement, even created a supergang of Dillinger, Baby Face Nelson and Pretty Boy Floyd, which allegedly robbed the Merchant's National Bank of South Bend, Indiana, on June 30, but the supergang was pure fiction. Floyd was hiding in Ohio, Nelson was in California at the time. No one has ever been charged for the robbery.

The big reward and the public's avid interest in him forced Dillinger into seclusion. He was afraid to show his face on the streets anywhere. He and his girl friend, Billie

Frechette, lived in a Chicago apartment, quietly staying out of sight. The public, eager for news, exhorted the FBI to find Dillinger.

The Barkers and Karpis were inactive, but Bonnie and Clyde were making headlines all over the Southwest. When the mad-dog lovers killed two Texas state motorcycle officers near Grapevine, Texas, on April 1, 1934, it marked the beginning of the end for the Texas-born outlaws. On May 23, on a country road near Gibland, Louisiana, a posse led by Texas ranger Frank Hamer ambushed the deadly pair. Thus ended the agonizing story of lovers who robbed, killed, and maimed as a way of life.

Bonnie and Clyde never received the wealth of public adulation other depression-era criminals enjoyed. Their murderous acts were too horrid even for the hero-starved citizenry. Regardless, their exploits attracted world-wide attention and sold a lot of newspapers. Psychologists explained it as a love theme that intrigued the public, much as the mother-son relationship of Ma Barker and her boys fascinated everyone. Bonnie and Clyde didn't become folk heroes until 1968 when a movie of their deeds was filmed.

In Los Angeles, Ed Davis discovered life going straight was tough. Work was scarce, and without identification, even scarcer. Once again, he was broke, so he resorted to the only way he knew to gain income, robbery. He held up a small store and kidnapped the proprietor, Gordon Windish, and another man in the store, J. J. Ball. Police apprehended Davis; he was tried and sentenced to Fulton prison on June 22, 1934, for life. The charge was three counts of burglary, first degree; six counts of robbery, first; and two counts of kidnapping. He was given Number 61175.

Kansas authorities placed a hold order on Davis, then closed the books on the last of the eleven Memorial Day escapees. If they could get Clark and Delmar, the second big break could be chalked off as well.

July was unusually hot for Chicago. Holed up all day, Dillinger and his girl friend skipped out for an occasional movie at night. Dillinger's buddy, Tommy Carroll, had been killed in Waterloo, Iowa, by a police officer on June 5, and the other gang members were scattered around the country. Dillinger was lying very low. But Chicago police were setting a trap for him. His landlady, a Roumanian immigrant who went by the name of Anna Sage, had agreed to accompany Dillinger and Billie to the Biograph Theater in exchange for freedom from a deportation order. Purvis okayed the plan for the FBI; East Chicago, Indiana, detective Martin Zarkovich and Chicago police captain John Stege collaborated. On the night of July 22, Dillinger was gunned down outside the theater.

Jim Clark and Delmar waited until two weeks after their escape to rob their first bank, taking the Goodland, Kansas, bank for $2,000 on February 9, 1934. During the robbery, Clark was shot in both feet by an officer who was on the ground under a car and could only see the bandits' feet. Clark was back in action by May 9, when he got $500 from the Wetumka, Oklahoma bank. Then on May 31, he returned to the Kingfisher, Oklahoma, bank he'd robbed with Bailey, Brady, and Underhill in August of 1933. On June 20, he struck the Crescent, Oklahoma, bank, then got $13,000 from the same Clinton, Oklahoma, bank he'd robbed the previous year with Bailey, Davis, and Underhill. Clark and Goldie Johnson were thought to have robbed the Oxford, Kansas, bank, but they denied having anything to do with that job. No one was ever charged for that robbery.

Major Wint Smith was hot on the trail all summer. Acting on the governor's instructions to spare no expense, Smith contacted Jim Bracewell, a former Texas ranger, who was working for the Texas Pipe Line Company. Living in Coffeyville, Kansas, Bracewell had been hired to stop persistent gasoline thefts from the pipeline, which ran above ground. It was common practice for thieves to "pinch" a line and haul away a load of gasoline. Bracewell agreed to help find Jim Clark.

Smith then took Earl Silverthorne off the regular state police roster and assigned him to the special "Clark" unit. Smith called in Major Ellis Christensen from Emporia, Kansas, Joe Anderson, another special officer, and John De-Long, known as an expert marksman, to complete the squad.

"Gentlemen, the governor has put a two-hundred-dollar price on Jim Clark's head and the state banking association has matched it," he told his stern-faced group. "Now go get Jim Clark."

An intricate plan was devised by Silverthorne and Christensen. Since Silverthorne was not well known as a lawman, having joined the force only recently after graduation from Kansas University, he was selected to be an undercover agent. Christensen would back him up as the contact man. The plan called for Silverthorne to meet Bob Brady's widow, Leona, figuring she would eventually lead them to Clark, whose girl friend Goldie was her close confidante.

The pair checked rumors, raided suspected hideouts, and were about to give up the search for Leona when they heard she was somewhere in Texas. It was common practice in the depression years for people with no permanent address to pick up mail at the general-delivery window. Arrangements were made with the Houston post office that in the event Leona called for her mail, a light above the window would be lit. The two officers took turns waiting in the lobby for weeks before the light went on one day. Silverthorne sized up the woman at the window, determined it was Leona, and followed her to a rooming house several blocks away.

Christensen, waiting outside the post office in a car, watched Silverthorne leave and followed him, making certain no one else was doing so. Silverthorne, an attractive, athletic man with, oddly enough, silver hair, took a room next to Leona in the boarding house. The widow was attractive, as well, and before long the pair met and began to date. When she complained about the conditions in the boarding house, Silverthorne found her an apartment. He had introduced himself as "E. H. Scott," and soon she was calling him "Scotty." He hinted strongly he was in the rackets and was an ex-convict.

Christensen reported daily to Topeka about Silverthorne's progress. Major Smith urged caution and advised the agents not to rush things.

One day, Leona suggested she was tiring of Houston and wanted Scotty to accompany her to friendlier Tulsa. Silverthorne's pulse quickened but he acted as if the idea had no appeal. Finally, she "talked him into it."

When Christensen phoned the good news to Smith, it was greeted with a cheer. If Clark was hiding in Tulsa, it was a certainty Leona and Goldie would get together. They hoped the bank robber wouldn't be far away.

Smith purposely kept the information from Oklahoma officials. He feared an informant might let the news out, or, worse yet, Oklahoma lawmen might attempt to capture the double-escapee themselves. Clark still owed time to the state of Oklahoma as well as Kansas.

Mrs. Brady took an apartment at 1335 South Peoria in Tulsa, a dozen or so blocks from the downtown area. Joe Anderson and Bracewell were dispatched to Tulsa, where they set up headquarters in the downtown Mincks Hotel.

One day in early July, Leona told Silverthorne she had some friends she wanted him to meet. He was confident this was the break he'd been waiting for so long. Christensen, who had not seen his family in six months, was delighted when he heard the news, feeling the case could be winding down.

Silverthorne, to further enhance his role as a racketeer and ex-convict, adopted a second alias in Tulsa, that of

"Charley White." Brady's widow still called him Scotty, however.

It was Tuesday, July 31, 1934, when the big break came. Mrs. Brady and Silverthorne drove to Nelagony to pick up Jim Clark's girl friend and her sister.

As Silverthorne drove into Goldie's place, his heart beat wildly. On the porch stood a wiry man about five feet eight inches tall and weighing about 140 pounds. The description fit Clark. As Leona and Silverthorne alighted from the car, the girls and Clark walked toward them. Clark extended a sun-tanned hand toward the agent, his icy blue eyes staring hard into Silverthorne's face. Apparently satisfied, he invited the secret agent in for a beer.

The day dragged on. Soon, "Charley Scott" began to talk about the beauties of Tulsa living, adding that he wasn't much of a "small town boy." The group agreed to drive into the big city, to Mrs. Brady's apartment, after first stopping for a watermelon feast on the way.

Clark parked his Ford, which he had purchased only two days before, in front of the Peoria Street apartment building.

Meanwhile, Bracewell, Anderson, and Christensen had decided to call for aid. Two Department of Justice agents, Paul Hanson and O. J. Hall, were summoned to sweat out the anticipated call from Silverthorne. Christensen sat uneasily at the phone, a machine gun beside him on a chair. Bracewell, a crack shot, sat cleaning and oiling an automatic rifle. Hanson and Hall both sat with machine guns nearby. Hall also had two .38-caliber automatic pistols within reach.

At the apartment, Clark's girl friend became uneasy. It was about midnight.

"Jim, I don't like this place. Something's wrong, let's get out of here," she told Clark. Silverthorne's hand tightened around the bottle of beer he was holding. Had he been discovered, or was the girl just wanting to go home?

"Oh, let's have something to eat," Leona volunteered.

She arose and walked to the kitchenette, opened the door of the icebox, and lifted out some lunch meat. She then discovered there was no bread.

"Scotty, will you go down to the corner and get some bread?" she asked. Silverthorne knew this was the break he'd been waiting for, but to avoid suspicion, grumbled and suggested someone else go. No one volunteered, fortunately, so he slipped on his suit coat to cover the shoulder holster he was wearing and walked to an all-night delicatessen two doors away. He borrowed the telephone, asked central to ring the number of the Mincks Hotel. Christensen eagerly answered.

"Chris, we're at the apartment, but you'll have to hurry. Clark may be leaving right away," Silverthorne spoke into the phone. He hung up, got the bread and some more sandwich meat, and returned to the apartment. He had to keep the outlaw there a while to permit the officers to arrive from downtown.

While Goldie continued to nag about leaving, Clark ate a sandwich, then arose to leave. Silverthorne glanced at his watch and knew he should stall another five minutes at least.

"Come on, Jim, have another beer before you go," he offered.

It was about 1:30 on the morning of August 1 when Clark and the others walked out of the apartment. As they stepped to the sidewalk, a car careened around the corner of Fourteenth Street onto Peoria. The occupants of the car drove past Clark and the two sisters, failing at first to recognize the escapee. Christensen whipped the car around the block and again approached the group. Clark, carrying an automatic pistol inside a newspaper, was fumbling with the door lock. In the glove compartment was more than $600, and he had carefully locked the car before going inside the apartment. As he swung open the car door and stepped back to let the girls in, there was a screech of brakes and three men leaped from a car beside the parked Ford.

Hanson, first out of the car, yelled, "Put 'em up. We're officers." He jammed the machine gun in Clark's side.

Clark stared at the officers. His girl friend, realizing the pistol was inside the newspaper, and that Clark would probably be killed if he tried to use it, threw her arms around the convict and screamed, "Give up, Daddy, give up."

"Don't start any funny business now, Jim," Hanson warned.

"All right," the outlaw said quietly and turned the pistol over to the officers.

Clark was led to the Kansas officers' car where Bracewell took the wheel and Christensen and Hanson sat on either side of the prisoner in the back seat. The other officers loaded the girls into their car and drove them to the Tulsa police station, where they were charged with harboring a fugitive and accessories to bank robbery. Incidentally, the charges were dropped several days later.

Bracewell pointed the car north, stopped briefly at the Mincks Hotel to phone the news to Wint Smith.

"Great," Major Smith responded. "I'll meet you in Sedan." Sedan is near the Oklahoma–Kansas line.

Bracewell, doubly afraid that Oklahoma officers would confiscate their prize or that Clark's buddies might try to free him, was driving like a man possessed. One time the car struck a bump and passengers were tossed about in the back seat. Clark, still wearing the straw hat he had on when captured, fell on Christensen and the hard brim of the hat struck the officer on the nose, causing a cut.

When Bracewell continued at breakneck speed, Clark tapped him on the shoulder and said, "I'm going to owe Kansas a lot of time and if you will slow down some, I may be able to serve at least part of it."

Clark looked at Christensen's bleeding nose and wryly

added, "Well, you can't say I didn't draw blood."

At Sedan, Major Smith anxiously awaited the arrival of his men. When Bracewell wheeled up, Smith immediately ordered Christensen to take the car on to Emporia and spend the night with the family he hadn't seen in six months.

"You be in Topeka tomorrow morning to take Clark on back to Lansing," Smith told him. Smith and several other officers whisked the convict on to Topeka for the night.

The next morning, Christensen escorted Clark to the prison. As they passed through Perry, Kansas, Clark wondered if the officer had a drink of whiskey.

"I'm gonna need one when I see those walls again," the Oklahoman commented. Christensen handed him a bottle and Clark took a long pull. He remained silent the rest of the trip.

As it turned out, Clark was not to remain at Lansing. Bracewell had succeeded in whisking him past the Oklahoma authorities and back to Major Smith, Governor Landon, and Kansas justice. But, under the new crime laws, Clark was also a federal offender. Although Kansas had initial jurisdiction, it allowed the United States district court in Oklahoma City to try Clark on the promise that, once convicted and sentenced, he would be returned to Kansas. The federal authorities reneged on the deal and Clark was sent to Leavenworth, a maneuver for which they would pay a hefty price in the years to come.

## The End of an Era

# 18

The reaction to Dillinger's death in Chicago was a shock to the FBI, which took considerable flak for its handling of the case. It was criticized for the "murder" of the killer, and for gunning him down "in cold blood" on the street instead of "bravely arresting him in his seat in the theater." It was chastised for using an informer, "the woman in red," to trap him. The bureau was stunned, believing it would gain acceptance by getting rid of the public enemy. Not everybody was on the side of the G-man.

But Hoover and his men dauntlessly carried on the crusade. Cowley and Purvis continued to concentrate on the kingpins of crime, Floyd, the Barkers, Karpis, and Baby Face Nelson, the strutting punk who had killed an agent in the Little Bohemia fiasco. The final months of 1934 would be monumental in the FBI's battle against crime.

Floyd had not surfaced for nearly a year except for a brush with police in Tulsa, where he was almost captured. Back with his wife, Ruby, Floyd had been trying to live a moral life and put his young son, Jack Dempsey Floyd, in school. One day, Floyd was recognized and barely escaped. Again, Ruby and the boy were separated from him as he fled to Iowa.

During this time, the FBI wrestled with the Union Station massacre case with little success. After a series of unsubstantiated allegations as to the killers, the bureau finally accepted Agent R. J. Vetterli's version of seeing "three men hunkered over" in the fleeing coupe at the massacre. Shortly after the shootings, agents raided Verne Miller's house on Edgevale Road in Kansas City and found Adam Richetti's fingerprints on some beer bottles. This, at least, put Richetti in Kansas City at the time of the massacre, although none of the dozens of witnesses identified a swarthy, five foot seven, 123-pound gunman at the scene. Pressured for some decision, the FBI finally announced that Floyd, Miller, and Richetti were the culprits. At least this officially excused Harvey Bailey, Jim Clark, Bob Brady, and Wilbur Underhill of any involvement in the botched-up attempt to release Nash.

Vetterli, who actually had seen Miller's coat thrown over the seat when the car sped away, was positive he had seen three men "hunkered over" despite the many witnesses testifying there had been only two men. Others, incidentally, said they'd seen up to seven men pulling triggers.

In earlier days, with George Birdwell as a partner (or sometimes acting alone), Floyd had established a reputation as a bank robber by nailing small Oklahoma banks in towns like Earlsboro, Paden, Castle, Sallisaw, Maud, Konawa, Morris, and Shamrock. He teamed up with Richetti shortly after Birdwell attempted to rob the bank in the all-black Oklahoma town of Boley and was gunned down on the street. Floyd had warned against a white man robbing a bank in an all-black town, but Birdwell and a friend, C. C. Patterson, and a black companion, Johnny Glass, walked into the bank in broad daylight. It happened on November

22, 1932, which was the opening day of the bird-hunting season. When the alarm was sounded, hunters took pot shots at the fleeing bandits and thousands of pellets were fired in their direction. Floyd had to seek a new running mate.

Richetti, living in Coalgate, Oklahoma, met Floyd for the first time in the town of Seminole, after Floyd, dressed as a woman, had attended Birdwell's funeral. Officers heard of the daring Floyd ploy and raided the house where Richetti, Floyd, and several others outside the law were staying. In the shoot-out, Richetti and Floyd escaped together, and the team was formed. Their first recorded crime was less than a week later, on November 30, 1932, when they held up a public dance at Wewoka, Oklahoma. The hall was filled with oilfield workers who had just been paid, and the loot was substantial. Later, the pair robbed the Farmers and Merchants Bank of Mexico, Missouri, on June 14, 1933, three days before the Union Station massacre. Following the robbery, they fled by car, eventually reaching Kansas City, where they ran into Verne Miller in the nightclub. They stayed the night of June 16 in Miller's home on Edgevale Road.

Following the massacre, Richetti and Floyd made contact in Ohio, where Floyd had a brother and sister living near Dillonvale. The nation-wide search for the Kansas City killers kept the pair out of circulation. The FBI concentrated even more on Floyd and Richetti after Miller's body was found on November 29, 1933, nude and trussed, alongside a country road outside Detroit. Miller, cracking under the stress, had begun drinking heavily, and the Purple Gang, which controlled Detroit's vice, didn't like the heat he brought with him. He was polished off in gangland style.

Almost a year later, on October 10, 1934, Floyd and Richetti were hiding in Iowa when officers flushed them. They fled to Ohio once more. On Friday, October 19, they robbed the Tiltonsville, Ohio, bank of $500 and fled north to a wooded area near Wellsville. The next day, a farmer reported two men camping near his home. Chief of Police J. H. Fultz and two special deputies drove to the area. When Fultz approached the men, lying on blankets, the suspects suddenly jumped to their feet and began firing at the officers. Fultz returned the gunfire and the men ran into the woods. The three lawmen gave chase and caught up to the men near a wooden building. Fultz fired a shot that struck the building just above one suspect's head, sending splinters flying into the air. The man threw up his hands in surrender, but his companion kept running. The captured man admitted he was Adam Richetti, but wouldn't acknowledge his companion's identity. Richetti had $98 in his pocket, which he claimed he'd won in a card game in Melina, Ohio.

Melvin Purvis in Chicago was notified of Richetti's capture and flew to East Liverpool immediately. He was rushed to Wellsville by auto where he began interrogating Richetti. Floyd was hiding in the woods.

On the morning of October 22, after two days in the woods, Floyd wandered onto the farm of Mrs. Ellen Conkle. He begged a meal from the farm woman, and offered her five dollars, which she refused. Unbeknown to the bandit, a farmer had seen him emerge from the woods and notified East Liverpool authorities. Purvis and two carloads of officers rushed to the Conkle farm.

Floyd finished his meal and then offered Stewart Dyke, Mrs. Conkle's brother, ten dollars to drive him to Youngstown. Dyke, claiming he had too many chores to do, refused, but agreed to take him into Clarkson, a nearby village. Dyke went to the barn to get the car. Dyke pulled the car to the front of the house, where Floyd and Mrs. Conkle, ordered to go along, entered the back seat of the old sedan.

As the car started down the lane that led to the county

highway, two cars turned into the drive. Floyd ordered Dyke to stop.

"Drive around behind that corn crib," Floyd ordered, waving a .45 pistol.

Behind the crib, Floyd leaped from the car and ordered Dyke to drive on. The brother and sister returned to the house as Floyd peered intently at the approaching cars in the lane.

Purvis and his men evacuated the cars in front of the house and began fanning out in all directions. Floyd broke from behind the corn crib and ran into a cornfield, most of the stalks harvested of the ears and flat on the ground. He made an easy target and a fusillade of bullets screamed in his direction. Suddenly, he stumbled to one knee, his back still to his tormentors. He pitched forward on his face, rolled over on his back, then on his face again. He struggled to his knees, but another bullet tore into his body and he fell forward. Officers ran to his side, removed the twin .45s, and handcuffed his hands behind his back. Purvis and FBI agent Herman Hawless were among the first to arrive at the outlaw's side. Another lawman on the scene was Chester C. Smith, an East Liverpool officer. At this point, the official FBI version of what happened and Smith's differ totally. Smith waited forty years, incidentally, to reveal what he said occurred.

Purvis said he asked the fallen criminal only two questions: "Are you Pretty Boy Floyd?" and "Did you have anything to do with the Union Station massacre?" Then, the agent said, Floyd died as the sun set in the Columbiana County hills.

Smith agreed that Purvis did ask those questions—and considerably more. The police officer said he was first to arrive beside the wounded Floyd, who appeared to have only a shoulder wound and another in the lower body. He was propped up on one elbow between the corn rows. When Purvis asked if he was Pretty Boy, the outlaw answered, "I'm Charles Arthur Floyd." To the Union Station query, Floyd said, "Hell, no. I wouldn't tell you sons of bitches anything."

Then, according to Smith, Floyd asked Purvis a question, "Where is Eddie?" obviously referring to Richetti.

Purvis responded that Richetti was in jail. There was a moment of silence.

Then, through clenched teeth, Floyd said: "You got me twice."

Purvis continued to quiz Floyd about the Union Station affair. Again, Floyd cursed the agent. Purvis, according to Smith, then turned to Agent Hawless and commanded: "Shoot him."

Smith said Hawless fired twice at Floyd, who was on the ground facing the agents at the time. One bullet tore into the breastbone, the other into the mid-section, Smith related.

Smith's allegation bears considerable credibility upon investigation. Floyd's mother, who drove to Kansas City to claim the body of her son after it was shipped from Ohio, looked sadly at the body and exclaimed, "There's something very strange about my son's death." She was probably wondering how he could have talked to the agents, as they stated, with a bullet hole through the heart area. She permitted no photographs of the body to be taken, however.

Floyd's body was taken to Akins, Oklahoma, and more than ten thousand people crowded the little town to witness the funeral. Curiosity seekers tried to pull the nails out of the pine coffin, and Pretty Boy's younger brother, who later would be Sequoyah County's sheriff for twenty years, knocked down a man trying to pull a splinter from the coffin. Again, Mrs. Floyd had forbidden cameras, and when she spotted a man in a tree in the cemetery trying to take a picture, she personally pulled him to the ground.

The saga of Pretty Boy ended in morbid fashion as the funeral developed into a circus.

The elimination of Floyd allowed the FBI to employ additional heat on the others. Baby Face Nelson was next, but he exacted a terrible toll before he died in a blazing shootout near Fox River Grove, Illinois, on November 27, 1934. Sam Cowley, the man who went after Dillinger, and Herman Hollis, another crack FBI agent, spotted Nelson on a country road and began a blazing gun chase that ended just outside the town of Barrington. Nelson, his wife, Helen, and John Paul Chase, a big-time bank robber, ran into a field to hide. The agents, armed with submachine guns, gave chase. Nelson, who copied many of James Cagney's movements from the movies, suddenly arose and, holding his machine gun at hip level, began walking toward the agents. Cowley fired his Thompson at the approaching gangster but to no avail. Nelson's bullets ripped Cowley apart. Hollis emptied his gun at Nelson, then turned to run. The bullets from Nelson's spraying machine gun cut Hollis almost in half. Helen and Chase ran to the side of the badly wounded Baby Face, placed him in a car, and roared away. The body was found in a ditch the next day near Hiles, Illinois, stripped to avoid immediate identification. Chase and Helen were captured less than a month later, thus closing another chapter in the fight against crime.

Unbelievably, the murders of Cowley and Hollis were underplayed by the press. Nelson's grandiose walk to destruction was magnified in true Hollywood style. The gangster-movie roles of James Cagney were personified in Nelson's dramatic death. Instead of mourning the demise of two brave men of the law, the public again berated the bureau. One newspaper actually called Nelson's death "the work of cowards." Still fresh in the public mind was Dillinger, and when Billie Frechette finished her jail time, she joined a carnival to tell folks about her lover. "He liked dancing, hunting, music and bread and gravy," she reported. Since bread and gravy was a staple depression meal, this struck a responsive chord with the public. Another newspaper printed a letter suggesting that "the FBI should have preached to the dead gangsters and instructed them to go and sin no more . . . to show a true Christian example."

An interview with Helen Gillis revealed that Baby Face died in her arms with a smile on his lips and tears in his eyes for his two young children. She failed to mention that she and Nelson had abandoned the youngsters years before, visiting them occasionally as "aunt and uncle."

Freddy Barker and Alvin Karpis, in a desperate attempt to disguise their features, paid a Chicago physician named Joseph P. Moran to alter their faces and fingertips. Every national magazine had published photographs of the Barker-Karpis gang, and they were afraid to appear anywhere. Dr. Moran's operations were totally unsuccessful and extremely painful. Moran was bumped off, buried in a pit, and lime tossed on the body. The remains have never been found.

Freddy Barker and Karpis then separated. Dock Barker was picked up on January 8, 1935, in Chicago by Purvis. The FBI rushed its prize to the offices, handcuffed him to a chair, and waited for him to talk. After eight days and nights, the exhausted agents gave up; Dock never cracked. There was a cell waiting for him on Alcatraz.

In Barker's apartment, officers discovered a map with the town of Ocala, Florida, circled. Investigation determined that the resort community on Lake Weir was where Ma and Freddy were quietly residing.

The agents descended on the cottage and demanded surrender. A burst of gunfire was the response. The withering fire of the agents blasted windows, doors, even mortar from the cottage. For forty-five minutes, bullets tore the cottage apart. After a five-minute respite, a black handyman who had worked for the Barkers was sent in to see if they were alive. He reported to those outside that "dey's dead." Purvis, again, was on the scene and led the agents inside where Freddy was found with eleven holes in his body, Ma with three. He was on the first floor, Ma was in an upstairs bedroom. The FBI issued a statement that Ma was discovered with "a smoking .300 gas-operated rifle" in her arms. Since there was at least a fifteen-minute delay following the cessation of shooting until the FBI entered the cottage, it was implausible the gun was still smoking.

The bodies were taken to an Ocala funeral home where they lay unclaimed for several months. George Barker, long separated from them, was scraping out a living as a filling-station operator in Carthage, Missouri, and didn't have enough money to have the bodies shipped home. Finally, with the cooperation of a funeral-parlor operator in nearby Welch, Oklahoma, the old man sent an ambulance to Florida to retrieve the nearly mummified bodies. He had them buried in a country cemetery six miles east of Welch in a remote area. Even in death the Barkers were ostracized, their plot being at least thirty feet from the nearest other gravesite.

The violent deaths of the Barkers didn't elicit much anti-FBI comment. But the Barkers and Karpis were never the public's favorites. Their crimes often involved persons, such as the Hamm and Bremer kidnappings, and there had been blood shed at many of their bank capers. At last, it appeared Hoover's lawmen were being accepted by the bulk of the populace. Courtney Ryley Cooper, the public-relations director of the FBI, was the unsung hero in the drive to gain popularity for the G-Man, and a national radio show and comic strip aimed at boosting the agents' image furthered the attempt. Karpis, now aware that he was the last remaining major target of the G-Men, laid low.

Hoover was still being needled about his ability to lead the nation's crime-busting agency because he had never made a personal arrest. So the director instructed his agents that when Karpis was eventually trapped, he was to be notified, regardless of the site. He would fly there and personally handcuff the new Public Enemy Number One.

Karpis was finally traced to New Orleans. He was shadowed for several days before Hoover was notified in Washington. When agents were positive they had Karpis cornered, Hoover flew to the Crescent City on May 1, 1936, to "make the arrest." Karpis was trapped in his car on a New Orleans street and surrounded by dozens of agents, each leveling rifles and pistols at him. He gave up without any sign of resistance. As he sat in the car, the word was passed to Hoover, standing beside a building, where he'd been watching the scenario unfold. He strode forward and "officially" arrested the killer, who sat casually in the car, wearing a mocking smile as the sham was being performed. When Hoover asked for a pair of handcuffs, there was great confusion among the agents. No one had thought to bring cuffs. One agent proffered his tie, which Hoover ceremoniously tied around Karpis's wrists. The FBI director had finally made an arrest!

Naturally, details of the arrest by the director were released to the press, although the official account didn't stress the use of a tie to manacle the public enemy.

The capture quieted most of the congressional criticism about the FBI's usefulness in the crime fight. From that point on, Hoover's power increased steadily and he became the most powerful behind-the-scenes person in government. He used his agency to compile dossiers on members of Congress and many other people, in and out of government. His reign would not end until his death. The dossiers would protect his position through the terms of six presidents, an unprecedented feat.

The capture of Karpis marked the end of the public's unnatural interest in the professional crime figures. The most dramatic symbol of this change was the opening of Alcatraz, in August, 1934. It effectively eliminated the threat of escape by big-name criminals. "The Rock" be-came a dreaded place for the criminal to contemplate, and any federal prisoner thought to be a trouble-maker was sent to the island in San Francisco Bay. All the big names of crime automatically went there, including Al Capone, Dock Barker, Machine Gun Kelly, Basil Banghart, Volney Davis, Harvey Bailey, Jim Clark, Albert Bates, Alvin Kar-pis, Dale Stamphil, John Paul Chase, and other hard-core cases. These men were deemed incapable of rehabilitation. In Alcatraz, prisoners were not allowed to talk except for a few minutes during exercise in the yard. The cruel "code of silence" was in force for the first six years of the prison's existence, until the convicts simply all began talking at one time during a meal, and the officials could do nothing. The rule was relaxed from then on. The terrors of Alcatraz were devastating. It was closed in 1964 after thirty years as a brutalizing maximum-security institution that took its human toll of inmates and guards alike.

By 1936, a light at the end of the depression tunnel could be seen, as FDR and his NRA became symbols of hope. Many of the failed banks re-opened. However, the new laws that brought many of them under federal protec-tion deterred a number of would-be robbers from entering the field so popular only three years before. Bank robberies, which peaked to a two-a-day average in 1932–34, dropped to less than one a week. In later years, population shifts away from the small farm communities made robbing banks with little deposits prohibitive for the risk involved. Radio-equipped police vehicles allowed road-blocking oper-ations even on remaining cat roads, thus negating their advantages as escape routes. It became easier to disappear in big-city traffic congestion than to run the cat roads.

The glamour of an individual criminal who happens to catch the public fancy is rare today. That period of the thirties when even minor bank robbers gained certain stat-ure among the American public was a one-time thing in history. It'll never happen again.

# Epilogue

## The Memorial Day Escapees

HARVEY BAILEY spent twelve years in Alcatraz before being transferred to Leavenworth on August 11, 1946. In 1960, as a first step toward returning to civilian life, he was assigned to the federal institution at Seagoville, Texas, a minimum-security prison. When he was finally paroled in 1962, the state of Kansas had a detainer against him resulting from his escape in 1933, and he was returned to Lansing. On March 31, 1965, he was paroled and accepted a job as a cabinetmaker in Joplin, Missouri. He was seventy-eight years old. When he was eighty-two, the strain of standing at a lathe became too great for his legs and he had to retire.

While in Leavenworth in 1948, he and his wife divorced, despite Bailey's conversion to Catholicism in Alcatraz. In 1966, he married the widow of Herb "Deafy" Farmer, who was sent to Alcatraz as an accomplice in the Union Station massacre because some of the telephone conversations between Hot Springs and Kansas City included him. Farmer, a part-time fence and arranger, had phoned various contacts in behalf of Frank Nash's wife, so he became part of the plot to free the captured outlaw. Farmer died in prison.

Bailey's amazing memory remained as steadfast as his hatred for J. Edgar Hoover, and he recalled minute details of his twenty-nine bank robberies with amazing clarity. In fact, in 1975, he re-ran the route he had taken on Memorial Day, 1933, most of the cat roads still in place where they were at the time of the break, but improved with asphalt or concrete paving.

When asked why he had never revealed to the FBI the details he had been told about the Union Station massacre, he snorted: "I'd never tell them sons of bitches anything." He blamed Hoover for his false imprisonment on the Urschel case.

On March 1, 1979, he died in a Joplin hospital after a series of kidney problems. He was lucid to the very end.

LEWIS BECHTEL served his remaining time in Lansing without incident and was paroled on June 25, 1939. He was granted a full pardon on January 11, 1941, and there is no further record of him or his whereabouts.

JIM CLARK became a cause of concern for the Department of Corrections. Although he never again attempted to escape confinement, prison officials probably wished that he had. When the United States government reneged on its promise to return Clark to the Kansas authorities after being tried on more serious federal charges, he was sentenced to ninety-nine years in the federal penitentiary at Leavenworth, where he was received on January 14, 1935. In 1937, he was transferred to Alcatraz. The code of silence was still in effect. Clark, certainly not a talkative type, decided to break the dehumanizing rule. He began a series of thrusts and parries at the system, some of which got him time in the dungeon on bread and water, but he persisted. Eight times he was charged with a variety of misdemeanors such as wasting food, causing confusion, talking in the mess hall, possession of contraband, causing confusion in the mess hall, causing confusion in the cell house, and breaking down discipline. There was little question his minor harassments were getting under the collective skins of the Bureau of Prisons. He was shipped back to Leavenworth, possibly the only man in the Rock's thirty-year history who "escaped" from Alcatraz by being a pest. At Leavenworth, from 1948 until 1958, he ruled the prison's gambling and loan-shark operations. Leavenworth wanted him returned to Alcatraz, which didn't want him back. The following letter was sent to the Department of Corrections by the Leavenworth warden:

"Jim Clark was placed in segregation on September 23, 1957 because of repeated rumors and circumstantial evidence that he was the "king pin" of all the organized gambling within the institution. For months, the officers have been convinced that Clark controls the gambling, financing all the bookies. However, he is a cunning individual on whom they have been unable to develop any conclusive evidence. He seems to have the ability to get large numbers of henchmen to do his dirty work, and when gamblers are caught, we have been unable to get any of them to identify Clark. However, a number of inmates who have become indebted to gambling to the point they have to demand protection, have identified Clark as the man who finances the bookies. He has been able to keep a group of strong arm artists working for him and keeps himself in the background. As further evidence that he is responsible, it should be noted that since he was placed in segregation, this type of activity has lessened to a marked degree. He and inmate Frank L. Lewing have operated in conjunction with each other. Lewing controlled the loan shark racket which thrived because of the gambling operation. Clark is an extremely cunning individual and knows the Leavenworth institution's physical plant extremely well. While the record indicates no disciplinary violations since 1952, he is definitely identified as the king pin in the gambling activities and has a strong influence among the inmates here and he cannot ever be safely returned to our population. He has already served over 22 years of a 99-year sentence, 13 of which were in Alcatraz. A transfer back to Alcatraz would not only provide the close supervision required to keep his activities under control, but relieve our crowded segregation unit."

So, once again Clark went to the Rock on January 14, 1958. Two years later he was back at Leavenworth, preparatory to parole. He had become an adept machinist and was in charge of maintaining the penitentiary's sewing machines. He was sent to Seagoville, Texas, to await parole and on December 9, 1969, was released. He became a ranch hand, then moved into a trailer home with his new wife. Clark married his deceased brother's ex-wife, Hazel Clark. They led a happy life and were saving some money from his new job in a small town in southern Oklahoma. It was typical of his wry style that he landed a job operating the parking lot for a bank. On his death, June 9, 1974, three of his pallbearers were bankers.

ED DAVIS, gradually losing his hearing, became known as "Old Deafy" in the state prison at Folsom, California, although he was only thirty-four when he arrived there on June 22, 1934. He despised Folsom because Warden Clarence Larkin ran a tight ship. Larkin, in fact, issued instructions that regardless of the circumstances or number of hostages in an attempted break, guards were to shoot to kill. Each Sunday, Larkin listened to inmate gripes and requests for parole. On September 19, 1937, Davis was among the forty convicts in line waiting to talk to the warden. Captain W. J. Ryan and Guard James Kerns stood at the warden's door to admit each prisoner. Suddenly, seven convicts broke ranks and rushed Ryan and Kerns, sweeping them into the warden's office. Larkin, forty-eight, was seated at his desk. He looked up to see Davis standing over him with a prison-made knife in his right hand. Davis ordered Larkin to phone the tower guards.

"Tell them to throw down some rifles," Davis screamed, brandishing the knife in the warden's face. In the outer office, the warden's secretary, Jack Whalen, heard the shouting and switched on the intercom. He immediately called the tower guards when he heard the commotion, the warden having eased on the switch as Davis threatened him.

Convicts Albert Kessel and Robert Cannon also had knives. The others, Fred Barnes, Ben Kucharski, Clyde Stevens, and Wesley Eudy, were unarmed.

Davis and Barnes grabbed the warden and shoved him toward the door. Whalen, remembering Larkin's instruction, told the tower guards to open fire once the convicts reached the prison yard. Another guard, H. D. Martin, was grabbed by the seven inmates and shoved into the yard. The tower guards held their fire until Stevens and Kucharski broke loose and ran toward the wall. A hail of bullets sent them crashing headlong onto the cinders. Davis and the remaining prisoners began slashing the hostages, the warden slumping to the ground with a dozen gaping wounds. Guard Martin died on the spot as the crazed convicts sliced and hacked with their homemade knives. The other guards, Ryan and Kerns, were bleeding profusely from their wounds when the five convicts suddenly threw away their weapons and held their hands high above their heads.

When the slaughter was over, Martin and Stevens were

dead. Kucharski was still alive, but succumbed several days later. Larkin was rushed to the hospital and for five days clung tenaciously to life. He was given five blood transfusions before he began to show signs of recovery. On the sixth day, he died of infection from the knife blades rather than the wounds themselves. Ryan and Kerns recovered. The five convicts stood trial and were sentenced to die in the gas chamber at San Quentin. On December 8, 1937, Davis entered "Q." He was the last to die. Kessell and Cannon went first, then Barnes and Eudy. Davis, always the loner, was once again a single act. Defiant to the end, he scribbled these last words: "No regrets for Old Ed. All considered, my conscience is now resting easy." The date was December 16, 1938.

CLIFF DOPSON was paroled from the Kansas penitentiary on March 6, 1936. He was released to the sheriff of Arkansas County, Arkansas. On July 16, 1936, he was received at the Missouri State Prison from St. Francoise County, on a robbery, first degree, charge, sentenced to 19½ years. He was pardoned in 1943. There is no further record of the St. Louisan.

HAROLD WESLEY "BILLIE WOODS" HARRIS led a troubled and violent life following his return to Lansing. Several times he was sent to the "hole" on bread and water, once for stealing malted-milk powder from the hospital and another time for having a homemade lamp in his cell. When first returned to the prison, Woods was put on the rock pile, but he continually quit work to chat with other inmates. Each time, he was slapped into isolation, yet he persisted. Then, in January, 1934, when he heard rumors of the impending Clark-Brady escape, he attacked another prisoner to get into isolation with the two plotters. When

Clark and Brady went over the wall, prison officials were unaware Woods and Dopson attempted to join them, but couldn't get Woods's cell door open. Woods was returned to his regular "B" house cell, but cursed a night attendant and was back on bread and water.

Woods had always been able to convince parole boards he had gone straight despite his dreadful record. Lansing officials let him go in 1936. He promptly stole a car and took it across a state line, a federal offense. He was sent to Leavenworth where again his persuasive powers gained a quick release. Lansing demanded him back as a parole violator, however. Finally, on February 28, 1941, he was granted a full pardon by Governor Payne Ratner's office.

A year later, he was picked up in Clinton, Illinois, for a burglary investigation by the DeWitt County sheriff's office, but released for lack of evidence. Using his real name of Harold Harris, he opened a hamburger joint on West Florissant Avenue in St. Louis, while living in the 5300 block of Bartmer Street. Earlier, while he was in prison, his wife, Anna, had lived in several different houses in the St. Louis area, first at 2719A North Tenth, then at 1225 Walton, and finally at Harris's sister's home at 1303 Warren.

Early one morning, a Missouri highway patrolman searched a car near Bluffton in Gasconade County, west of St. Louis, following a report of a break-in in the little community. Harris had a complete arsenal in the car—rifles, pistols, and shotguns. He was convicted of burglary and grand larceny and given an eight-year sentence. Unbelievably, he was paroled in less than two years.

Again using the name of Woods, he moved to Kansas City, Kansas, where he got a job selling cars for Feld Chevrolet. But there were so few cars being allowed the public during World War II years, he returned to St. Louis, driving one of the demonstrator cars he forgot to turn back to the agency. Failing to find work because of his prison record, he decided to revert to his real name again and move to Eminence, Missouri, which is the heart of a rugged area known as "the Wilderness." He set up housekeeping on a farm, supplying game for the table with his sharpshooting ability with a rifle.

"Every shot he took got meat," a neighbor indicated.

Harris and a new wife, named Delores, settled into the rustic life well and soon had two daughters. In 1950, Barbara Wanda was four and Retta Mae was two. Harris had become well known in the hill country and was living an honest life from all appearances.

Harris began to show great interest in the fifteen-year-old daughter of a neighbor, R.N. Fansler. Young Lola Jean Fansler did not share the affection, so Harris drove to the Fansler farm one day and abducted the young girl. No one was home at the time, and the Fansler's weren't sure what happened to Lola Jean until Harris arrived the next morning demanding her clothing. His wife and two daughters had gone to the Fansler house seeking him the night before and had been invited to spend the night. As Fansler and Harris argued in the living room, Mrs. Harris and Mrs. Fansler waited in the kitchen. Homer Fansler, twenty-one-year-old brother of Lola Jean, and his girlfriend, Joyce Thomas, sixteen, entered the living room just as Harris reached for a .32-caliber pistol in his pocket. The elder Fansler started to protest, but one shot sent him sprawling to the floor. Homer jumped on Harris's back and attempted to wrest the gun from the ex-convict's hand. The two women rushed into the room after hearing the shot, and Elmer Nichols, Mrs. Fansler's brother who was working in the barn, started running to the house at the same time. As the men wrestled for the gun, two shots were accidentally fired. One struck little Barbara Wanda and killed her instantly. The second hit Mrs. Fansler and she fell to the floor, screaming. With a sudden jerk, Harris freed the gun and shot Homer Fansler in the head, killing him instantly. Harris saw his daughter's body on the floor and ran to her side. He lifted her into his arms, still holding the pistol in his right hand. Just then, Nichols entered the door. A shot struck Nichols in the hip, sending him crashing backward to the porch floor. Harris ordered his wife and Joyce Thomas to accompany him, and he ran to his car, carrying his daughter. Less than a mile from the shooting scene, Harris skidded the car into a ditch and it became mired. Leaving the women and his child's body in the car, he ran into nearby woods and disappeared.

The state highway patrol descended on the area and established roadblocks. Two days later, on August 9, 1950, Harris saw a truck drive away from a road block on a dirt road in the heart of the timberland and, thinking the post was being abandoned, crossed the road. The driver of the truck had gone for sandwiches while two deputies remained at the roadblock, unseen by Harris. Deputy Paul Frey called for Harris to halt. The startled killer leaped behind a tree instead. Frey, also a crack shot, waited for Harris to peer around the tree and picked him off with one shot. Burial was in New Picker Cemetery, St. Louis.

Lola Jean was found unhurt in an abandoned barn.

ALVA "SONNY" PAYTON, although blinded by the shotgun blast in the aborted bank robbery at Altamont, Kansas, survived his wounds and served until granted a parole in 1936. He and his wife, Leota, tried unsuccessfully to make a living selling Avon products, belts, leather goods, and other products door to door. He then filed for a blind pension, which was denied, as he had not been an Oklahoma resident for five consecutive years at the time. Leota tried to get on the WPA works program, but the rolls were filled. In desperation, they turned to making moonshine whiskey, a common practice in dry Oklahoma. A son was born to the couple and their monetary needs increased. Payton learned to read and write Braille and could operate a standard typewriter keyboard, but wasn't able to get a job using those skills. Federal alcohol and tax agents swooped down on their illegal whiskey operation, and on August 14, 1941, the Paytons were sentenced. Alva got a two-year prison term and $100 fine on one count, thirty months in federal prison on a second count. Leota got ten months on each count. She was sent to Seagoville, Texas, to serve her time; he was sent to Leavenworth. Sometime after his release he moved to Portsmouth, Virginia, where he had relatives, and was later reported living in Fort Wayne, Indiana, with other relatives. No further information has been recorded.

FRANK SAWYER'S case turned out to be the most bizarre of all. After being captured in Oklahoma following the break from Lansing, he was returned to McAlester to finish his sentence there. He was transferred to the state reformatory in 1946, paroled to Kansas officials to finish his interrupted sentence there. On September 18, 1969, he was granted a full pardon when it was determined he, Ed Davis, and Jim Clark had been falsely imprisoned since 1932 on the Fort Scott heist. Sawyer was released to a nephew from Odessa, Texas. When a Kansas City television newsman, Charles Gray, reminded Sawyer, who was seventy at the time, that the state of Oklahoma had a detainer on him for the Union, Oklahoma, bank and post office robbery in 1932, he detoured around the state on the drive to Texas. He spent several years with nephews in Odessa and Midland, Texas. One day a niece answered a telephone call from a woman in Chicago, who said she was Frank Sawyer's daughter and was trying to locate his grave. The niece, unaware that Sawyer's wife had told the daughter her father had died years before, informed the caller that Sawyer was "sitting right here." The happy daughter rushed to Texas to see the parent she thought she would never know.

As a result of the false imprisonment, Sawyer sued the state of Kansas, but the case was never resolved.

## Companions in Crime

ARTHUR "DOCK" BARKER, while in Alcatraz, attempted to escape on June 13, 1936, along with Dale Stamphil. The pair eased into the water and were forced back onto the rocky shore by the strong tides. As they hid among the rocks, a guard boat shone a spotlight on them. According to officials, the pair attempted to run, and were gunned down, Barker dying of a bullet wound in the head, Stamphil receiving bullet wounds in both legs. But according to Stamphil, Barker was shot when he peeked above one of the rocks, the bullet entering the skull at an angle, leaving him unconscious and bleeding but not dead. Guards placed both men in a rowboat that was being towed by the larger boat.

"Dock was alive and moaning, but no one even looked at his wound," Stamphil reported. "They carefully placed my head next to the big boat's exhaust and if the wind hadn't shifted about the time I ran out of breath, I would have been asphyxiated. When we got to the hospital, we were put on beds, but neither of us were seen by a doctor. Dock moaned all night long and didn't die until fourteen hours later. They finally treated my legs, after four days when I hadn't bled to death as they'd hoped."

Stamphil lives in Kansas City, Kansas, and works with inmates at Leavenworth in an alcohol treatment program and is a member of the state's rehabilitation counseling board. He has been given full pardon by the federal and Kansas governments.

Barker is buried in a private cemetery in San Francisco used for Alcatraz inmates who died there, the only identifying marker being his prison number on the metal tablet above the grave.

GEORGE "MACHINE GUN KELLY" BARNES died in the penitentiary at Leavenworth in 1954. He had also served considerable time on Alcatraz. Kelly's cellmate at Leavenworth, Willie Radkay, who now lives in Prescott, Kansas, remembers that Kelly, who had heart trouble, had eaten a meal of beans the night before a fatal heart attack. Although he had what he considered "gas pains," Kelly felt reasonably well for a fifty-seven-year-old inmate, Radkay recalls.

"Then I got a call out in the yard that he was having pains, but he died before I got back to the cell. Old Man Shannon down at Paradise, Texas, sent the money for his burial and he was shipped to the family plot there."

ALBERT BATES died in Alcatraz and he, too, is buried in the San Francisco cemetery where plots were reserved for prisoners.

FRED "KILLER" BURKE, the member of the massacre squad in the St. Valentine's Day murders in Chicago in 1929, who was hidden on Harvey Bailey's farm in Missouri until picked up in 1932, spent the rest of his life in the Michigan state prison, convicted of murder. Burke, who accumulated a large amount of wealth for a man in his profession, was allowed to live almost like a king in his cell, since it was permissible for people who could afford it to have luxuries brought in. Burke became corpulent and, a diabetic, literally ate himself to death.

VOLNEY DAVIS, the long-time Barker gang member, died in 1978 in Oregon after a long illness. He had suffered from arthritis, undoubtedly worsened by his years on the cold and damp island prison in San Francisco Bay.

FRANK DELMAR, Jim Clark's running mate on the second escape attempt, died in Leavenworth about 1957.

LARRY DEVOL, a member of the Fort Scott robbery gang and of the Barker-Karpis gang, served time in Alcatraz (under the name Larry O'Keefe) along with Karpis.

TOMMIE HOLDEN, half of the Evergreen bandit team, wound up in Alcatraz. When finally released, he went to Chicago and, while drunk, killed his wife, mother-in-law, and sister-in-law. He fled to the state of Washington, where he was apprehended and returned to Illinois. He was sentenced to the state prison for the killings and died there some time later of a heart attack.

FRANCIS KEATING, the other half of the Evergreen bandit team, at last word was still alive and residing in Florida.

ALVIN KARPIS spent from August 7, 1936, until 1962 in Alcatraz, then was transferred to the McNeil Island federal penitentiary. In 1969 he was paroled and deported to his native Canada. He moved to Spain, where he died of an apparent overdose of drugs in 1979.

JACK "TOM" LLOYD, one of Underhill's henchmen, died in the federal corrections hospital facility at Springfield, Missouri, where he had been transferred from Alcatraz for treatment of a skin disease.

ADAM RICHETTI, following his capture in Ohio two days before his companion Pretty Boy Floyd was gunned down, was returned to Kansas City and charged with the Union Station murders as well as those of two officers near Columbia, Missouri, on June 14, 1933, three days before the massacre. He was found guilty in both cases and sentenced to die. Richetti protested his innocence to the end. Oddly, two weeks before his scheduled execution, two brothers walked into patrol headquarters and admitted they had slain the two officers at the roadblock. With that portion of the death sentence erased, Richetti felt he might escape the gas chamber since the flimsy evidence of his participation in the Union Station massacre was all that remained. His appeal was denied and he was taken to the gas chamber in the Missouri state prison on October 7, 1938. As the straps were being tightened around his arms and legs, he raised his eyes upwards and yelled: "What have I done to deserve this?" A guard instructed him to breathe deeply when the fumes reached his face, but Richetti, struggling with his bonds, took one large gasp of the lethal gas and issued an ear-piercing scream. Bob Debo, a reporter and one of the chosen witnesses of the execution, claimed he heard the shattering scream for years afterward.

## Lawmen and Others

WINT SMITH, who headed the Kansas state police under Governor Alf Landon, later became a United States congressman from the Sunflower State and was a well-respected political leader for many years. He died in 1977.

ELLIS CHRISTENSEN, who was in on the chase for Jim Clark, is still living in Emporia, Kansas, but his fellow officer, EARL SILVERTHORNE died in the forties.

R. J. VETTERLI, one of the survivors of the Union Station massacre, was transferred to the FBI's San Francisco office shortly after the killings. He then shifted to St. Louis, succeeding Lear B. Reed, who later became chief of police of Kansas City. Before he died of a heart attack at forty-five years of age on June 16, 1949, almost sixteen years to the day after the massacre, he served in FBI offices in Philadelphia, Atlanta, Birmingham, New York, and Norfolk, Virginia.

KIRK PRATHER, the Kansas state prison warden who was kidnapped by the eleven escapees on Memorial Day, 1933, ran unsuccessfully for the Democratic gubernatorial candidacy in 1934, then disappeared from public life. He died of a heart attack in 1939, at the age of fifty-six.

JACK STEWART and JOHN VAN METER, the two youngsters who sat in the stands with their fathers watching the ball game when the break occurred, still live in the Lansing area. Stewart, an accountant, has an office within the shadows of the penitentiary wall, and Van Meter, after a long military career, returned to the prison as personnel officer in the early seventies.

VIRGINIA WOODSON, the fifteen-year-old girl who drove the family car confiscated by the escapees, also still lives in Lansing. Her married name is Huggins. Her younger brother, Robert, who was fishing nearby at the time of the break, later became warden of the prison until a change in state politics caused him to resign.

ALMIRA UNDERHILL, mother of Wilbur, died on October 1, 1951, in a Kansas City hospital at the age of eighty-one. In 1948, she was named "Mother of the Year" by the Heart of America chapter, National Secretaries Association, of which the hard-working sister of Wilbur, Dorothy, was a member. Dorothy died in 1971 while working as a secretary for the Kansas City liquor control department. She was sixty-six.

Wilbur's brother George, who died of a drug overdose in 1931, is buried alongside him in the family plot in Memo-

rial Park, Joplin. So is his brother Ernest, who died of cir-
rhosis in 1937.

MIKE FANNING, the police officer at the Union Station who
fired the shots at the fleeing killers following the massacre,
wound up an inmate at the Missouri State Penitentiary.
Several years after the massacre, Fanning got drunk one
night and killed a fellow officer. He was sentenced to Jefferson City and soon became a trusty, assigned to drive a
car for one of the prison officials. He was seen some time
later in front of the Hotel Muehlebach in downtown Kansas City and was relieved of his trusty rank. Following his
discharge several years later, he returned to Kansas City.

# Index

**Billie Woods**

**Cliff Dopson**

**Lewis Bechtel**

**Sonny Payton**

```
SAWYER, FRANK              KSP 298
REG. 7-8-32      BIRTHDATE 5-1-9
CRIME BANK ROBBERY HAB.
SENTENCE 20-100
HEIGHT  5' 11"      HAIR    GRAY
WEIGHT  165         EYES    BROWN
BUILD MEDIUM        RACE    WHITE
REMARKS:   REMUGGED 12-18-62
```

**Frank Sawyer**

**Wilbur Underhill**

**Harvey Bailey**

**Bob Brady**

**Jim Clark**